ROUGH GUIDES

POCKET
SHETLAND

written and researched by
OWEN MORTON

CONTENTS

Introduction 4

When to visit.. 6
Where to.. 7
Shetland at a glance..................................... 8
Things not to miss...................................... 10

Places 23

Lerwick and around..................................... 24
Bressay and Noss.. 34
South Mainland.. 40
Fair Isle.. 52
Central Mainland... 56
Westside... 64
Northeast Mainland..................................... 74
Whalsay and Out Skerries........................... 80
Northmavine.. 86
Yell... 94
Fetlar.. 100
Unst.. 104

Accommodation 115

Essentials 121

Arrival 122
Getting around... 122
Directory A–Z.. 124
Festivals and events................................. 128
Chronology.. 129
Language 131
Small print.. 132
Index 134

SHETLAND

INTRODUCTION

The archipelago of Shetland, more than 100 miles north of the Scottish mainland, and famously closer to Bergen in Norway than to Manchester, is a beautiful and quite unique destination. Its rugged coastline offers a seemingly endless choice of routes for gorgeous walks, as well as excellent wildlife-spotting opportunities, while the rich history of these islands has left many outstanding archeological sites to explore. On top of all this is the fascinating Shetland culture, which takes influences from its Norse heritage just as much as the Scottish, resulting in remarkable festivals such as the fire-focused Up Helly Aa which are quite unlike anything found elsewhere in the UK. It may take a little bit of effort to get here, but it's well worth it: Shetland is quite simply enchanting.

Norwick beach on the island of Unst

Shetland is formed of about 100 islands, but only 16 of them are inhabited. The majority of the 23,000 inhabitants live on the largest island, known as Mainland, with more than 6,000 people in Shetland's capital and largest town, Lerwick. There are other reasonably large settlements found on Mainland, including Scalloway – the capital until the eighteenth century – and Brae, but for the most part the rest of Shetland's population live in fairly small villages and hamlets, mainly along the coastline.

The archipelago has an extremely long history, with evidence of inhabitation dating back to around 4300 BC. Early sites on Shetland include the Scord of Brouster, a collection of Neolithic-era houses, and Stanydale Temple, so named because of its resemblance to prehistoric religious sites on the Mediterranean island of Malta. Shetland's most impressive prehistoric site, though, is Jarlshof, found at the southern tip of Mainland, which not only holds the remains of Bronze Age houses but also evidence of almost every subsequent archeological era until the seventeenth century.

During the Iron Age (from around 500 BC), some of Shetland's most iconic buildings were constructed: the brochs. At 13 metres tall, the Broch of Mousa is the best preserved example in Shetland – and indeed in the world – but there are countless others across the archipelago, although their purpose remains unknown.

In the following centuries, Shetland was occupied by the Picts, but by the eighth century raids from Vikings – pushing westward from nearby Norway – were becoming ever more common. At some point around 800 AD, the Vikings arrived to stay, ushering in more than 600 years of Norse rule. Across the archipelago you'll come across archeological remains of Viking settlements, with their distinctive longhouses found in particular concentration on the northern island of Unst, and there is enduring evidence of the Norse years in many place names across Shetland: anywhere with a name ending -wick, for example, is derived from the Old Norse 'vik', meaning 'bay'.

As Scotland's power grew, there was intermittent interest from its kings in adding Shetland to their territory, with a brief war in the 1260s over the issue. In the event, though, the Norse era came to an end through diplomacy, in 1462, when the daughter of Christian I of Denmark and Norway married James III of Scotland: Shetland and Orkney were pawned to Scotland in lieu of a dowry. Although the Norwegians intended to eventually settle the bill and recover the Northern Isles, continuing to raise the issue until the 1660s, from this point on Shetland was firmly established as Scottish territory.

The political situation notwithstanding, Shetland's economy in this era was booming, thanks to trade with the powerful Hanseatic League. Merchants from northern Europe would make the journey across to Shetland and trade in böds (warehouses) for salt fish, bringing goods and currency.

What's new?

One of Shetland's most exciting new initiatives is the Wild Skies Trail (www.wildskiesshetland.com) in Unst, the northernmost of the islands. The trail criss-crosses Unst, with interactive information panels set up at some of the island's top sights, inviting the visitor to explore aspects of its culture, history and heritage from different perspectives.

Nobody puts Shetland in a box

In 2018, the Scottish Parliament passed the Islands Bill which, among other things, made it illegal for public bodies to put Shetland in a box on maps, instead requiring them to display the islands "in a manner that accurately and proportionately represents their geographical location in relation to the rest of Scotland". This change reflected the opinion of many islanders, who felt that presenting Shetland in a box misrepresented the distance between Shetland and mainland Scotland.

Until 1707, when trade with the Hanseatic League was outlawed, Shetland saw visitors from many nations and used Dutch currency just as freely as Scottish. Several Hanseatic-era böds survive in Shetland, including a particularly well-preserved one on Whalsay.

The eighteenth century saw the rise of the haaf fishing system, in which men would head out to sea in large six-oared rowing boats (known as sixareens) and remain some distance from shore for several days. When they returned to dry land, they put in at haaf stations, where other workers (usually older men and boys) would set to work curing the catch, preparing it for export. The system was extremely exploitative, with landowners making large profits, while fishermen livied at subsistence level. The haaf system only ended around 1900, when larger boats made it uneconomical.

Shetland played an important role in World War II, when its proximity to Scandinavia made it ideal for running undercover assignments to German-occupied Norway. Based out of Scalloway and known as the Shetland Bus, these secret missions smuggled resistance fighters onto the continent and rescued fugitives, at great personal risk to the British and Norwegian operatives. In the 1970s, Shetland's economy was boosted by the discovery of North Sea oil and the subsequent construction of Sullom Voe Oil Terminal. Tourism too has become an important industry, with visitors drawn by its stunning coastline, outstanding wildlife-spotting opportunities and fascinating history – and, of course, the chance to seek out locations used in the popular BBC crime series *Shetland*. With such varied attractions, Shetland is a destination which rewards a lengthy visit.

When to visit

The weather in Shetland can come as a surprise. It's a long way north – on the same latitude as St Petersburg in Russia and Churchill in Canada – but it never gets nearly so cold, thanks to the warming effects of the Gulf Stream. It can, and does, get pretty wet and windy though, whatever time of year you're here, so come prepared with waterproofs.

Summer and early autumn are the best seasons to come to Shetland, at which time you have a good chance of enjoying lovely sunny weather, and at midsummer you'll experience the famous 'simmer dim': a night-long twilight at which time the islands never get truly dark. At the other end of the year, winter may not seem an obvious time to visit, given the short days and generally inclement weather, but if you're hoping to experience any of Shetland's iconic fire festivals, notably Lerwick's Up Helly Aa, this is the time to come.

Where to...

Shop

Perhaps Shetland's most iconic product is Fair Isle knitwear, a style of knitting used in the creation of distinctive jumpers, hats, scarves and more. Its heritage can be explored at Fair Isle's George Waterston Museum and the Shetland Textile Museum in Lerwick, but you'll find it for sale in numerous locations across the islands, notably at Jamieson's in Lerwick and Nielanell in Hoswick. There's also a small but thriving jewellery industry to be found across Shetland, with a particular emphasis on silver pieces. Art lovers may want to check out Britain's most northerly art gallery, the Shetland Gallery on Yell; and products of the UK's northernmost gin distillery, on Unst, may also take your fancy. Lerwick's Commercial Street is a good place to browse many of these fine Shetland-based souvenirs.

OUR FAVOURITES: Jamieson's of Shetland, see page 32; Nielanell, see page 51; Esme Wilcock Jewellery, see page 93; The Shetland Gallery, see page 99.

Eat

There's excellent food to be found on Shetland, with local produce – particularly fish and seafood – taking centre-stage, but outside the larger settlements, places to eat can be few and far between. The greatest concentration of restaurants by far is found in Lerwick, where you can enjoy everything from fine dining to cheap and cheerful fish and chips, via a good selection of international offerings. Outside Lerwick, you'll find a smattering of cafés and restaurants, with hotels also offering evening meals. On the islands, options are considerably more limited: some, such as Fair Isle and Whalsay, have no permanent places to eat, while others have only one or two choices, which may be unexpectedly closed. On the other hand, many of the more remote communities operate pop-up takeaways: as you travel around the islands, you're likely to see signs advertising an upcoming fish and chips or Chinese evening in a village hall, and there are plenty of Shetland's iconic honesty box cake fridges to be found even in the remotest places.

OUR FAVOURITES: No 88, see page 33; Da Haaf, see page 63; Busta House Hotel, see page 79; Frankie's Fish and Chips, see page 79.

Drink

Shetland has very few pubs, perhaps owing to a 1920s archipelago-wide vote in which the majority of areas opted to go dry. Licensed premises began to reappear across Shetland from the 1940s, but there remains a relative lack of drinking establishments. Lerwick is the hotspot, with a number of lively places, including the traditional Douglas Arms and the modern Da Noost, but you'll also come across small and friendly bars in Scalloway, Brae and elsewhere – don't miss the Balta Light, the UK's most northerly pub, on Unst. For non-alcoholic drinks, there are plenty of cafés in Lerwick and several to be found elsewhere across the islands, including some very good tearooms.

OUR FAVOURITES: The Douglas Arms, see page 33; Da Noost, see page 33; The Original Cake Fridge, see page 73; The Kiln Bar, see page 63; The Balta Light, see page 113.

Shetland at a glance

Unst p.104.
Top of the list for Shetland's Viking heritage, the unmissable Unst is also home to gorgeous beaches, a spaceport, and a famous bus stop.

Yell p.94.
Shetland's second largest island is home to one of its finest beaches, the Sands of Breckon, as well as a beautiful coast walk to the Broch of Burraness.

Northmavine p.86.
An ancient volcanic past has resulted in Northmavine's splendid jagged coastline offering some of Shetland's best walks, including the cliffs of Esha Ness.

Northeast Mainland p.74.
The gateway to the Northern Isles offers stunning coast walks, including the popular route at Muckle Roe and rugged paths at Lunna Ness.

Westside p.64.
Get your walking boots on for a hike along some of Shetland's most beautiful coastal scenery at Deepdale, or explore archeological sites such as Stanydale Temple.

Central Mainland p.56.
Explore Shetland's past at the former capital of Scalloway, relax on beautiful sandy beaches, or pay a visit to iconic Shetland ponies.

Fair Isle p.52.
Alone in the North Sea directly between Shetland and Orkney, Fair Isle is one of Britain's most isolated islands and an ideal place to watch seabirds.

Fetlar p.100.

The 'Garden of Shetland', Fetlar is an attractively green island with fine cliff walks and an imposingly gothic nineteenth-century ruined mansion.

Whalsay and Out Skerries p.80.

Head to Whalsay to check out its significant prehistoric remains and Britain's northernmost golf course, or to the Out Skerries for Scotland's most eastern point.

Lerwick and around p.24.

Explore Shetland's picturesque capital, taking in the outstanding Shetland Museum and the seafront Lodberries, an iconic filming location in the BBC's *Shetland* series.

Bressay and Noss p.34.

Across the harbour from Lerwick, Bressay offers attractive walking country, while the smaller island of Noss is one of Shetland's best places to spot marine wildlife.

South Mainland p.40.

Head south to some of Shetland's top sights, including the remarkable archeological site of Jarlshof and the iconic double-sided beach of St Ninian's Isle.

15 Things not to miss

It's not possible to see everything that Shetland has to offer in one trip – and we don't suggest you try. What follows is a curation of Shetland's highlights, from archeological wonders to the best beaches, coastal walks and wildlife viewing.

> **Esha Ness**
See page 90
Ancient volcanic activity has produced some of Shetland's most stunning coastline, with jagged black rocks onto which the sea crashes dramatically.

< **Jarlshof**
See page 49
Shetland's top archeological site, with remains from every era of settlement from the Bronze Age to the seventeenth century, Jarlshof offers Shetland's entire history in one place.

∨ **Up Helly Aa**
See page 27
Shetland's foremost fire festival, held in Lerwick in deepest winter, is a cultural experience unlike any other.

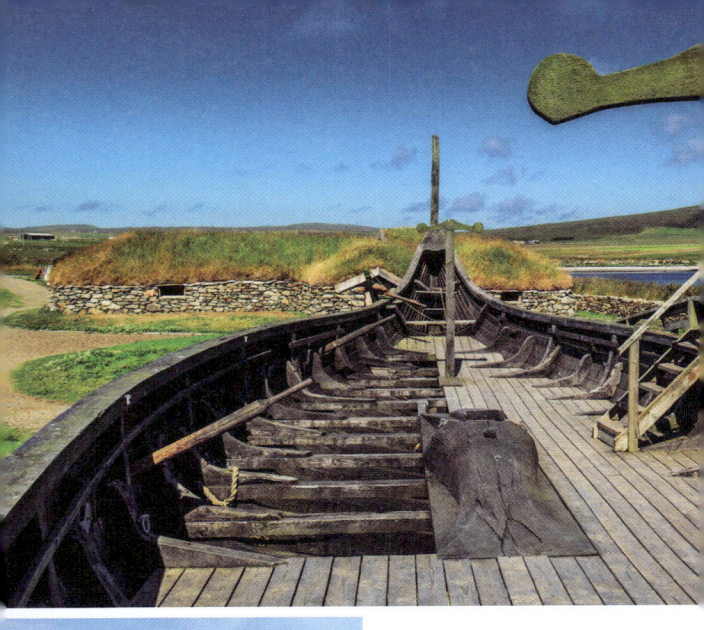

< **St Ninian's Isle**
See page 46
A remarkable double-sided beach known as a tombolo leads to St Ninian's Isle, a small island on which a hoard of Pictish treasure was discovered.

∨ **Broch of Mousa**
See page 44
The best-preserved broch in the world, this enormous prehistoric stone construction on the small island of Mousa resembles a cooling tower.

13

< Unst Viking Project
See page 110
Explore Shetland's Viking heritage on the northern island of Unst, at a reconstructed turf-roofed longhouse and a marvellous replica longboat.

∨ Shetland Pony Experience
See page 62
Learn about the iconic Shetland pony, before taking a group of them for a walk and a photoshoot on a picturesque beach.

THINGS NOT TO MISS

∧ Deepdale
See page 70
Get your hiking boots on for a walk along the gorgeous coastline of Westside, past bays and inlets overlooking the unexpectedly turquoise waters of the North Atlantic.

< Wildlife-watching at Sumburgh Head
See page 50
The southernmost point on Shetland's Mainland is ideal for keeping an eye out for marine life, including orcas and dolphins.

∧ Breckon Sands
See page 98
Shetland has plenty of pretty beaches, but Breckon Sands may just take the top spot: it's a gorgeous stretch of sand backed by attractive grassy dunes.

∨ Shetland Museum
See page 24
Engagingly laid-out and packed with fascinating exhibits, there's no better place to get an understanding of Shetland's history and culture.

∧ Hermanness Nature Reserve
See page 111
A walk on Hermanness offers a splendid stroll along Unst's jagged coastline, plenty of chances to spot marine life, and a view of the UK's most northerly point.

< Scalloway
See page 57
Shetland's former capital is home to an imposing castle and a marvellous museum exploring the town's World War II heritage.

17

< Culswick Broch
See page 71
A ruined broch atop a small hill is the destination for a lovely walk with outstanding views of Shetland's rugged coastline.

∨ Noss
See page 39
A dedicated nature reserve, the island of Noss is one of the best places in Shetland to go wildlife-watching: look out for seabirds, seals and orcas.

THINGS NOT TO MISS

Day One in Shetland

Jarlshof. See page 49. Kick off your trip to Shetland with a trip through its history at Jarlshof, an archeological site boasting remains from almost all of Shetland's historical eras.

Sumburgh Head. See page 50. Visit the southernmost point on Shetland's Mainland to explore the lighthouse museum, keeping an eye out for marine life such as orcas in the surrounding waves.

Lunch. See page 51. Head to *Hoswick Visitor Centre* and enjoy an excellent light lunch, before checking out the interesting museum.

St Ninian's Isle. See page 46. Take a walk across the iconic tombolo beach to St Ninian's Isle, and if you're feeling energetic, extend the outing by walking around the island.

Shetland Museum and Archives. See page 24. Head north to Shetland's capital, Lerwick, and explore the fascinating museum to understand the archipelago's history and culture.

Dinner. See page 32. Take your pick from Lerwick's restaurants: good choices include *No 88*, which offers excellent local produce, or *C'est La Vie* for French and Spanish-influenced seafood.

The Lodberries. See page 29. Enjoy a leisurely after-dinner stroll along Lerwick's seafront to the iconic Lodberries, a run of gorgeous stone houses right on the water's edge.

Jarlshof

Shetland Museum and Archives

The Lodberries

Day Two in Shetland

Scalloway. See page 57. Head to Shetland's former capital to check out the imposing sixteenth-century castle and learn about the wartime Shetland Bus operations.

Hillswick Seal Sanctuary. See page 87. Take a trip onto the Northmavine peninsula and visit the seals at the Hillswick Seal Sanctuary to learn about these endearing Shetland natives.

Lunch. See page 93. Continuing westward, stop to enjoy a hearty lunch at the *Braewick Café*, with gorgeous views over the dramatic coastline.

Esha Ness. See page 90. This is one of Shetland's finest walks: take an amble along the beautifully rugged cliffs watching the powerful waves crash onto the rocks below.

Tangwick Haa. See page 87. If you have time, call in at the Tangwick Haa Museum to get an insight into rural Shetland culture.

Dinner. See page 93. Head back to Hillswick and tuck into an excellent meal in the Viking-themed dining room of the *St Magnus Hotel*.

Hillswick. See page 87. Walk off dinner with a stroll on Hillswick's short but attractive seafront, keeping an eye out for seals in the bay.

Seals on the shore

Tangwick Haa Museum

Hillswick seafront

The Northern Isles

Even this far north, you can always go norther... Take the ferries to Yell and Unst to explore the Northern Isles, home to some of Shetland's most spectacular scenery.

The White Wife. See page 95. Take the early ferry across to Yell and head to the island's east coast, for a short walk to the White Wife, the figurehead of a German ship that ran aground here in the 1920s.

The Sands of Breckon. See page 98. Drive up to Yell's northern coast and take a stroll on the Sands of Breckon, possibly Shetland's prettiest beach.

Bobby's Bus Shelter. See page 109. After crossing by ferry to Unst, head to Baltasound and take a quick look at Britain's most celebrated bus stop.

Lunch. See page 113. Either grab a cheap and cheerful sandwich at the *Final Checkout café*, or visit *Victoria's Vintage Tea Rooms* to linger over lunch while enjoying fine views over the bay.

The Unst Viking Project. See page 110. Continue to Haroldswick and explore Unst's Norse heritage at the reconstructed longhouse and the majestic replica Viking longboat.

Hermanness. See page 111. Take a walk along the Hermanness peninsula, from the northern tip of which you'll have a view across to the rocky island of Out Stack, which is the northernmost point of the British Isles.

Dinner. See page 113. If they're serving food, enjoy pub grub at the *Balta Light*, Britain's most northerly bar. Otherwise, see if your B&B can offer an evening meal.

The White Wife

Sands of Breckon

Bobby's Bus Shelter

Budget Shetland

Although it's not cheap to get there in the first place, once on the islands it's possible to take in much of what Shetland has to offer without spending large amounts of money.

Historic Shetland. A couple of Shetland's top sights, including Jarlshof, charge for entry, but the vast majority of the archipelago's historic sites are free to visit. On Mainland, the Broch of Burraland, the Ness of Burgi, Stanydale Temple, and the haaf fishing station at Fethaland, as well as Lerwick's Shetland Museum, are all excellent choices, and all the Viking remains on Unst are free as well.

Walking. One of the principal reasons to visit Shetland is to take in its marvellous walking routes, and these can all be done for free. Routes such as the cliffs at Esha Ness, the coastal path to Deepdale and the gorgeous walk to Culswick Broch are just the start: there are enough hikes, both long and short, here to keep you busy for days without the need to spend anything.

Wildlife spotting. Shetland is a splendid place to spot wildlife: keep your eyes peeled and you have a decent chance of seeing otters, and along the coastline there are seals aplenty as well as seabirds in large numbers. The waters are also home to marine life such as orcas and dolphins, among much else: although wildlife-watching boat trips aren't free, there's no charge for looking out from the shoreline.

Practicalities. Shetland's B&Bs and hotels tend to err towards the pricey end of the scale, but consider either wild camping or staying over at campsites to keep costs down. Food and drink can be expensive too, so opt for self-catering and stock up in Lerwick for picnic lunches.

Historic water mill on Muckle Roe

Stile at Esha Ness

An orca offshore

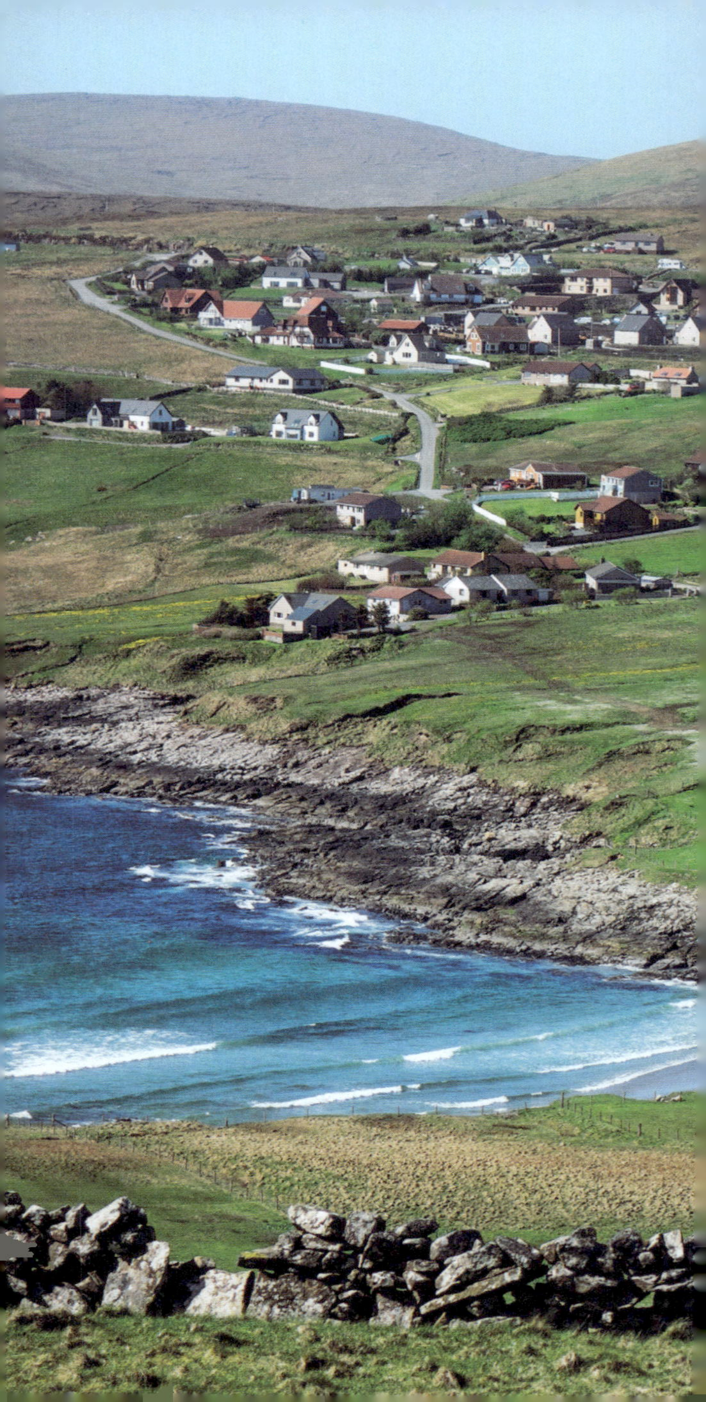

PLACES

Lerwick and around	**24**
Bressay and Noss	**34**
South Mainland	**40**
Fair Isle	**52**
Central Mainland	**56**
Westside	**64**
Northeast Mainland	**72**
Whalsay and Out Skerries	**78**
Northmavine	**84**
Yell	**92**
Fetlar	**98**
Unst	**102**

Gulberwick

Lerwick and around

Shetland's capital, Lerwick, is by far the largest settlement on the archipelago, and is home to many of the best restaurants and shops, as well as a decent range of accommodation. It's an attractive town, particularly along the waterfront and in the picturesque alleys that wind off the pedestrianised Commercial Street. Must-see attractions include the Shetland Museum, which offers an excellent overview of Shetland's history and culture, and the excellent Iron Age ruined Broch of Clickimin, found on the town's outskirts. For lovers of the *Shetland* TV series, the town is also a great place for some location spotting.

Hay's Dock

MAP PAGE 26
Hays Dock, Lerwick, ZE1 0WP. Free.
First built in 1815, Hay's Dock is the sole remaining section of Lerwick's original docks. Throughout the nineteenth and twentieth centuries, it was a thriving area, but went into decline from the 1980s. It was redeveloped in the early 2000s, and is now home to the Shetland Museum and Mareel. Take a wander along the harbour front and enjoy the views out over Bressay Sound. The large propeller blade in between Mareel and the Museum was salvaged from the White Star Line ship *Oceanic*, which ran aground off Foula in 1915. Parts of the ship can be found across Shetland in plenty of museums, businesses, and even private homes.

Shetland Museum and Archives

MAP PAGE 26
Hays Dock, Lerwick, ZE1 0WP. http://shetlandmuseumandarchives.org.uk. Free.
This fantastic museum makes an excellent first port of call if you're hoping to get acquainted with the wealth of history that Shetland has to offer. Arranged chronologically, the galleries span two floors and begin with the region's geological formation, before moving into prehistory and the arrival of humans in Shetland, perhaps 6000 years ago.

Displays of artefacts found in chambered tombs and Stone Age sites give way to the Iron Age, with a fascinating exhibition on the uniquely Scottish constructions known as brochs, and then onward

Shetland Museum and Archives

Lerwick's harbour

to the Pictish and early Christian periods. Don't miss the magnificent display of silver treasure, found at St Ninian's Isle in 1958, including brooches and some beautifully ornate bowls.

The Viking and medieval periods enjoy extensive coverage, after which the museum enters the 1700s, from which there are many surviving ethnographic artefacts: farming and fishing were the two main livelihoods at the time, both well represented here.

Shetland's relationship with the sea has a particularly engaging section: look out for Shetland's oldest boat, a sixareen under which you can walk to admire its construction, and nearby, another sixareen in a marvellous state of preservation.

Upstairs, engaging exhibitions cover the nineteenth and twentieth centuries, with a focus on everyday life – music, fashion, shopping, the postal service, and the like. The changing economics of Shetland also gets an interesting display, from whaling and farming to the oil industry and tourism. If the Up Helly Aa Exhibition (see page 28) is closed, the section on the festival here will help to fill the gap – check out the fascinating video footage of Up Helly Aa events from years gone by.

Back downstairs, make sure to pop your head in to see what's on in Da Gadderie, which hosts temporary exhibitions. Afterwards, pop by the gift shop where there's a range of souvenirs available, from books to hand-made crafts.

Mareel

MAP PAGE 26
Gutters Gaet, Lerwick, ZE1 0WQ. http://shetlandarts.org/venues/mareel. Free.
A striking modern building on the waterfront, Mareel is a cinema and community hub, at which live music, talks and events are hosted. In 2021, *Time Out* magazine

Lerwick Centre

Bressay Sound

RESTAURANTS AND CAFÉS
C'est la Vie	2
Da Steak Hoose	5
The Dowry	3
No 88	4
Raba	1

ACCOMMODATION
Eddlewood Guesthouse	5
The Grand Hotel	2
Islesburgh House Hostel	3
Norlande Guest House	4
Rockvilla Guest House	1

SHOPS
Island Larder	3
Jamieson's of Shetland	4
Lerwick Distillery Shop	1
The Puffin Republic	2
The Shetland Times Bookshop	5

PUBS
Da Noost	2
Douglas Arms	1

Hay's Dock · Mareel · Shetland Islands Council · GUTTER GAET · MITCHELL'S RD · Shetland Museum and Archives · COMMERCIAL ROAD · Viking Bus Station · ST OLAF STREET · ST MAGNUS STREET · MARKET STREET · FORT ROAD · MILL LANE · COMMERCIAL ROAD · HARBOUR STREET · Out Skerries · Bressay · Esplanade Ferry Terminal · St Margaret and the Sacred Heart Church · Lerwick Police Office · Garrison Theatre · Fort Charlotte · AITKENS PLACE · ANDERSON PLACE · CHARLOTTE STREET · KING HARALD STREET · King George V Park · KING ERIK STREET · ST OLAF STREET · LOWER HILLHEAD · HILLHEAD · Lerwick Town Hall · HILL LANE · BURNS WALK · ESPLANADE · COMMERCIAL STREET · Victoria Pier · Playing Fields · PITT LANE · REFORM LANE · BANK LANE · HANGCLIFF LANE · LAW LANE · IRVINE PLACE · Market Cross · The Tolbooth · QUEENS LANE · Bain's Beach · UNION STREET · Shetland Library · KING HARALD STREET · PRINCE ALFRED STREET · Islesburgh Community Centre · Adam Clarke Memorial Methodist Church · HILLHEAD · MOUNTHOOLY STREET · CHURCH ROAD · NAVY LANE · GARDIE PLACE · SCALLOWAY ROAD · THORBIN ST · ANNSBRAE PLACE · RONALD ST · GREENFIELD PLACE · KNAB ROAD · St Columba's Church

| 0 | metres | 100 |
| 0 | yards | 100 |

ranked it Number 25 in a list of the world's most beautiful cinemas. Drop by to see what's on while you're in town.

Fort Charlotte

MAP PAGE 26
179 Commercial St, ZE1 0HX. http://historicenvironment.scot/visit-a-place/places/fort-charlotte. Free.

The squat, grey stone walls of Fort Charlotte sit ominously above the Bressay ferry terminal, with cannons pointing across the water ready to repel an approaching enemy and defend Lerwick's harbour. The star-shaped fort was built in 1661 and assumed its present form after reconstruction in the 1780s. Although it never saw any enemy action, rumours of its strength did deter a potential Dutch attack in 1667, and it was put to other uses across the centuries, including a customs house and a jail. Today, you can stroll around its massive walls, enjoying commanding views of the sea, harbour and town.

Lerwick Town Hall

MAP PAGE 26
Hillhead, ZE1 0HB. http://shetland.gov.uk/lerwick-town-hall. Free.

The gloriously Gothic town hall, just uphill from Fort Charlotte, was built in 1883, at a time when Lerwick was experiencing a boom

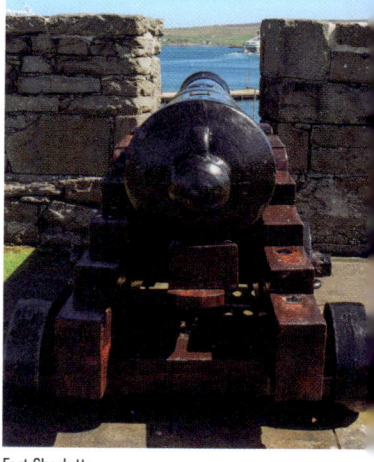

Fort Charlotte

from its fishing industry. Although the exterior is worth a look, it's really the inside that rewards a visit: the windows in the main hall are considered some of the UK's finest secular stained glass windows, depicting scenes from Shetland's Norse-era history in exquisite detail. As the town hall is still in use for the local council, you may not always be able to get inside, but if you call by during office hours you'll usually be able to come in for a look at the windows.

Up Helly Aa

On the last Tuesday in January, Lerwick plays host to Up Helly Aa, the largest of the fire festivals held in Shetland. Around nine hundred torchbearing participants, in extraordinary costumes, march in procession before throwing their torches into a longship. A firework display follows, then the squads do the rounds of a dozen 'halls' (including the Town Hall), giving comic performances at each. Since its inception in the 1880s, the participants had all been male, but in 2024 a squad included four women for the first time.

Up Helly Aa dates from Victorian times, and although it's essentially a community event with entry by invitation only, visitors are welcome at the Town Hall – visit http://uphellyaa.org for details.

Shetland Library

MAP PAGE 26

Lower Hillhead, ZE1 0EL. http://shetland.gov.uk/libraries. Free.

Should you wish to research any aspect of Shetland – whether it be history, geology, wildlife, industry, or anything else besides – the library is the place to come, with its dedicated Shetland room containing thousands of books on virtually any subject you could name.

King George V Park

MAP PAGE 26

King Harald St, ZE1 0EN. Free.

A block west of the town hall is the small, well-kept King George V Park, where you can enjoy a stroll around the paths admiring the pretty flower displays. It's perhaps not a town highlight, but worth a visit if you have time to spare.

Up Helly Aa Exhibition

MAP PAGE 26

Off St Sunniva St, ZE1 0HL. http://uphellyaa.org/up-helly-aa-exhibition. Free.

Only open throughout the summer months – and even then only at limited times – the Up Helly Aa Exhibition offers a glimpse behind the scenes of Shetland's famous fire festival. The exhibition includes plenty of photos and videos of events past, as well as outfits worn by recent squads.

Commercial Street

MAP PAGE 26

Commercial St, ZE1 0EX. Free.

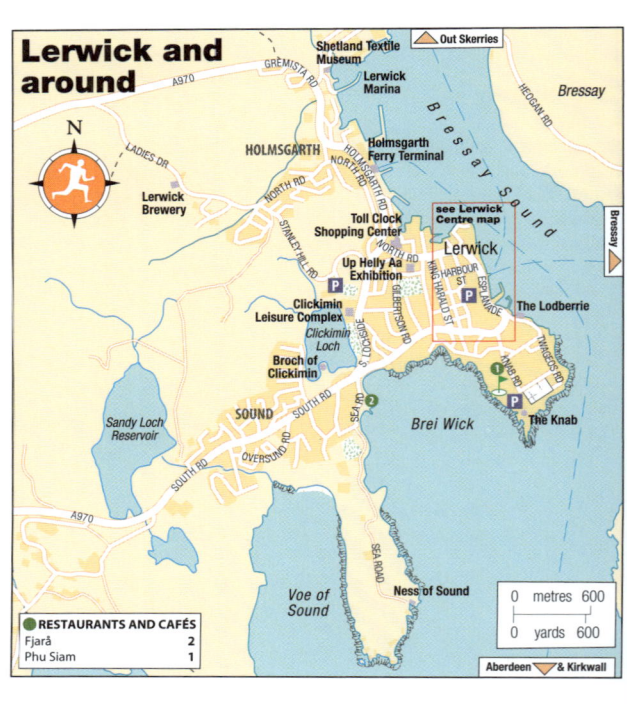

Running parallel to the seafront's Esplanade, Commercial Street is a largely pedestrianised, rather quaint street with attractive old buildings housing the majority of Lerwick's shops. It makes a very pleasant walk from the base of Fort Charlotte to the Market Cross. The narrow alleys running either side of Commercial Street are known as the Lanes: they're an atmospheric echo of how Lerwick looked in the nineteenth century.

Market Cross
MAP PAGE 26
Commercial St, ZE1 0BD. Free.

In an attractive little square stands the Market Cross, a small monument from which the Up Helly Aa celebrations kick off. Embedded in the cross's pillar is a barometer, a sign noting that it was lent by London's Meteorological Office, though it looks like it's been here long enough that it's unlikely to be returned.

Until November 2024, the square was also home to the incredibly helpful Tourist Centre, which was closed by VisitScotland as part of its drive to move services online. At time of writing, there was a possibility that it might be taken on as a local initiative; if it is open during your visit, you'll find it a valuable resource in navigating Shetland's sights, checking what's open, how to book ferries, and much more besides.

The Tolbooth
MAP PAGE 26
24 Commercial St, ZE1 0AB. 01595 693827. Free.

Found at the eastern end of the Esplanade, the Tolbooth is a handsome and substantial building with a clock tower perched on top. It dates from the 1770s and, as the name suggests, was originally used for tax collection. It's now considerably more popular, as it's the headquarters of the RNLI. Just outside is Da Lightsome Buoy, a monument to the many years of Shetland's fishing industry.

The Lodberries
MAP PAGE 26
20 Commercial St, ZE1 0AN. Free.

Derived from the Norse term *hlad berg*, meaning 'flat stone', the Lodberries are a run of gorgeous stone houses built right onto the seafront. One of them in particular

Commercial Street

draws visitors: just round from the small and sandy Bains Beach, it's used as a filming location in the *Shetland* TV series.

The Knab
MAP PAGE 28
Knab Rd, ZE1 0YB. Free.

Walking about a kilometre along Lerwick's sea front from the Lodberries, you'll reach the Knab, a finger of land pointing out to sea. It offers fine views across to Bressay, with the island's lighthouse easy to spot, as well as down the southern Mainland coast. Thanks to its commanding position over the entranceway to Lerwick's harbour, it was long used as a watch point, and the remains of military installations from both World Wars can still be seen around the point. A short and easy walk leads northwest from here back to town between the golf course and the sea: keep an eye out for seals on the rocks as you go.

Broch of Clickimin
MAP PAGE 28
South Rd, ZE1 0RD.
http://historicenvironment.scot/visit-a-

Shetland's böds

The stone buildings known as böds were originally built as basic accommodation for fishermen, and can be found across Shetland. Although some are now museums, many are still used for their original purpose – as places to sleep overnight. They're cheap, but very basic: you'll need to bring your own bedding, and note that they don't all have electricity.

place/places/clickimin-broch. Free.
On the western outskirts of Lerwick you'll find Clickimin Loch, on the edge of which is the Broch of Clickimin. It's an impressive Iron Age structure dating back to around 400 BC, and would originally have been around ten metres high. Brochs were built using a double-skinning technique, resulting in very thick walls with an interior gap, and Clickimin is an excellent place to see this architectural style in action: if you enter the centre of the broch, climb the staircase and head through the opening in the wall, you can see the interior passageway.

The purpose of building brochs remains unclear, but as Clickimin is surrounded by extensive ruins of outer walls and other buildings, the indications are that it was at the centre of a thriving community. However, there is also a theory that they had a ceremonial purpose: here at Clickimin, a flat slab of stone was found with life-sized footprints carved into it, which may have indicated where a participant in rituals should stand. The footprint slab is still here: look for it in the pile of stones in front of the broch's entrance, protected from the elements by another flat slab balanced above it.

Ness of Sound

MAP PAGE 28
Sea Rd, ZE1 0RN. Free.
A pleasant circular coastal walk of about 90 minutes, taking in some interesting World War II remains and offering the chance to see wildlife, starts from a car park accessed from the corner just as Sea Road bends inland. From the back of the car park, head through a gate and then simply follow the path around the peninsula, taking in a view of Bressay ahead and with the Knab to your left across the harbour. Seals can often be seen in the water and on the rocks here.

Within about ten minutes, you'll reach the World War II gun battery, installed to defend the harbour. Derelict now, you can explore its gun rooms and concrete passageways, some of them containing street art which

The Lodberries

Broch of Clickimin

varies greatly in quality. Afterwards, continue around the cliff edge, ascending to a point where you can see South Mainland stretching out ahead of you. Descend the other side, past cliffs home to nesting seabirds, and bend round with the coast heading back north.

At the top of the peninsula are the Sands of Sound, a lovely stretch of white sand and clear sea. Enjoy some time on the beach before picking up the path again to head inland, and turn right when you reach a road. At the top of a slope, turn right onto a wide gravel track and follow it round as it descends the other side of the peninsula. Walking around the sports field to the right will bring you out onto Sea Road; follow it to the right to the car park.

Shetland Textile Museum
MAP PAGE 28
Gremista Industrial Estate, ZE1 0PX.
http://shetlandtextilemuseum.com. Charge.
Housed in a well-preserved and atmospheric fishing böd outside the town centre to the north, the Textile Museum has three rooms covering the various styles of textile production found in Shetland. Downstairs is dedicated to weaving, with an enormous loom taking pride of place, while upstairs there's a display of Shetland lace pieces and Fair Isle knitwear. If you're a knitter yourself, you can contribute to Da Muckle Gravit (The Big Scarf), which was begun in 2004 and has been a work in progress by museum visitors ever since, reaching more than 60 metres long at time of writing. The museum's shop is a great place to pick up scarves, hats, jumpers and gloves.

Lerwick Brewery
MAP PAGE 28
Ladies Dr, ZE1 0NA.
http://lerwickbrewery.co.uk. Charge.
The Lerwick Brewery is home to Shetland's only craft beers, producing a range of tipples you'll find in bars across the islands. To learn more about how they're made, book onto one of the tours, which take you through the brewing process and end in the taproom where you can taste the products. Advance booking is essential.

Shops

Island Larder
MAP PAGE 26
97 Commercial St, ZE1 0BD.
http://islandlarder.co.uk.
Both café and shop, Island Larder has been around for some time but has become very popular after going viral on TikTok. You'll find coffee, tea and hot chocolate to drink, and you're almost certain to be tempted into some locally made ice cream, Scottish tablet, or the enticingly named Puffin Poo chocolates.

Jamieson's of Shetland
MAP PAGE 26
93–95 Commercial St, ZE1 0BD.
http://jamiesonsofshetland.co.uk.
If it's wool you want, you've come to the right place. There's every colour you can conceive of here, produced in the Jamieson's mill in Sandness in Shetland's west. You'll also find a fine selection of jumpers and other knitwear, should you not wish to buy the raw materials to make your own.

The Shetland Times Bookshop

Lerwick Distillery Shop
MAP PAGE 26
32 Market St, ZE1 0JP.
http://shetlandwhisky.com.
There are grand plans afoot to open the Lerwick Distillery for tours and tasting sessions at some point in the future, but in the meantime, you can visit the distillery shop to pick up a bottle of the very mellow blended whisky, as well as Shetland knitwear and other souvenirs.

The Puffin Republic
MAP PAGE 26
112 Commercial St, ZE1 0HX.
http://tinyurl.com/PuffinRepublic.
If you're looking for a Shetland souvenir, the Puffin Republic is a good place to start, with goods ranging from puffin-themed tea towels, coasters and art prints to Viking helmets.

The Shetland Times Bookshop
MAP PAGE 26
71–79 Commercial St, ZE1 0AJ.
http://shop.shetlandtimes.co.uk.
This excellent bookshop in the heart of Lerwick stocks an outstanding selection of Shetland-focussed titles – covering local history, geology, hiking, knitting, ponies, and plenty of Ann Cleeves – as well as books of wider Scottish interest, and more general fiction and non-fiction sections. Perfect for picking up some holiday reading.

Restaurants

C'est La Vie
MAP PAGE 26
181 Commercial St, ZE1 0HX.
http://facebook.com/Cestlavielerwick.
At lunchtime, C'est La Vie offers not only a good selection of French choices, but also a fine range of Spanish tapas. In the evening, the focus is on fish and seafood, with excellent options including Shetland Bouillabaisse and sautéed scallops. There's also a daily

changing catch of the day menu. It's advisable to book ahead. ££££

Da Steak Hoose
MAP PAGE 26
5 Mounthooly St, ZE1 0BL. http://facebook.com/lerwicksteakhouse.
Having been named Scotland's Steakhouse of the Year several times, this excellent restaurant serves up not only delicious steaks, but other enticing options such as seafood linguine or pork fillet stuffed with black pudding. If you have any room left, the sticky toffee pudding is spot on. £££

No 88
MAP PAGE 26
88 Commercial St, ZE1 0EX. http://no88shetland.com.
One of Lerwick's top restaurants, No 88 has a regularly changing menu based on seasonal local produce. Naturally, it makes good use of the abundant fish and seafood found in Shetland, but it's equally strong on meaty options, with local lamb dishes being particularly good. The Sunday lunches are legendary. £££

Phu Siam
MAP PAGE 28
20 Knab Rd, ZE1 0AX. 01595 694351.
The restaurant in the Glen Orchy House hotel serves authentic and very good Thai food, both stir fries and curries. The duck *pad kra pow* is an excellent choice. They also have a selection of Thai beers, which make a perfect accompaniment. £££

Raba
MAP PAGE 26
26 Commercial Rd, ZE1 0LX. 01595 695554.
One of several Indian restaurants in Lerwick, Raba is a no-frills place serving all the old favourites and several less common options, such as Railway Lamb Tava and Chicken Murag Bhaja, both of which are highly recommended. No alcohol served. ££

Cafés

The Dowry
MAP PAGE 26
98 Commercial St, ZE1 0EX. http://thedowry.co.uk.
Popular café-restaurant serving tasty comfort food, such as burgers, nachos, chicken wings and macaroni cheese. Leave some room for the salted caramel churros or apple gyoza. It's also open just for drinks, offering several beers from Lerwick Brewery. ££

Fjarå
MAP PAGE 28
Sea Rd, ZE1 0ZJ. http://fjaracoffee.com.
Get yourself a seat by the floor-to-ceiling windows and soak in the lovely views across the bay toward the Knab peninsula from this great café. The coffee and cakes are very good, as are the more substantial lunch or dinner options. ££

Pubs

Da Noost
MAP PAGE 26
86 Commercial St, ZE1 0EX. 01595 693377.
A popular nightspot with a vibe that successfully blends traditional bar with a touch of contemporary industrial. The bar is well stocked with a fine range of spirits, including the local gins from the northern island of Unst.

The Douglas Arms
MAP PAGE 26
67 Commercial Rd, ZE1 0NL. http://tinyurl.com/DouglasArms.
A real place of two halves: turning left on entry will bring you into a fairly uninspiring sports bar, but if you take the right-hand door you'll find yourself in an excellent local pub, with a lively and welcoming atmosphere, a great selection of beers and whiskies, and Viking shields resplendent above the bar. Live music on a Thursday night.

Bressay and Noss

The island of Bressay sits directly opposite Lerwick, and makes an easy day trip from Shetland's capital. It offers some interesting archeological sites, particularly the church ruins at Cullingsbrough, but the island's attractive and easy walking territory is perhaps a greater draw: walks along the south coast near the lighthouse are especially beautiful. During the summer months, you can also use Bressay as a stepping stone to the smaller island of Noss, a short hop from Bressay's eastern coast, which is one of Shetland's best places to see seabirds.

Bressay Heritage Centre

MAP PAGE 36
Bressay, ZE2 9EL. http://bressay.org/visit/heritage. Free.

Conveniently right at the ferry terminal, the Bressay Heritage Centre can give you an overview of what Bressay and Noss have to offer before you set off exploring. The exhibition touches on many topics of local interest, but particular highlights include some fascinating information on the Cruester Burnt Mound, and a reconstruction of a typical 1960s Bressay living room, which offers an enjoyable contrast to the many reconstructions of 1800s houses you'll see across Shetland.

Cruester Burnt Mound

MAP PAGE 36
Bressay, ZE2 9EL. Free.

Burnt mounds are Bronze Age structures which appear to have been used for heating stones in fire and then dropping them in water to create a high temperature – but

Ward of Bressay

Getting to Bressay and Noss

Ferries to Bressay leave Lerwick from the terminal beneath Fort Charlotte, though they're not as frequent as you might expect, averaging one per hour. The crossing takes about ten minutes, and carries both foot passengers and cars. To reach Noss, you'll need to head to the eastern shore of Bressay, where a foot ferry operates on demand between May and August, every day except Monday and Thursday.

we don't know what was then done with those high temperatures. Cooking and bathing are both possible uses, among others. This particular burnt mound originally stood several kilometres to the north, but was saved by the Bressay History Group from being washed away by the sea. Impressively, it was dismantled and painstakingly reconstructed in its present location outside the Heritage Centre.

Mail
MAP PAGE 36
Bressay, ZE2 9DH. Free.

Bressay's principal village is Mail, just south of the ferry terminal. It is home to the island's shop and café, and also has a picturesque little harbour, where you can often see seals relaxing on the rocky shore.

Ward of Bressay
MAP PAGE 36
Bressay, ZE2 9ER. Free.

The Ward of Bressay is the island's highest point. It can be climbed from a track leading from the end of a road called Upper Glebe, in the village of Mail. It's an easy route to follow – just make for the TV tower at the summit. Once you get there, you'll be rewarded with lovely panoramic views.

Fisherman's Memorial
MAP PAGE 36
Bressay, ZE2 9ER. Free.

A side road leads down to the coast just outside the village of Ham, at the end of which is a small monument to the eight fishermen who lost their lives during the years of the Ham Fishing Project between 1880 and 1914, when this settlement briefly took up small scale herring fishing. The project was already in decline from around 1910, and the outbreak of World War I comprehensively ended the industry.

Garth's Croft
MAP PAGE 36
Bressay, ZE2 9ER. http://garthscroftbressay.com. Charge.

A visit to Garth's Croft gives you the opportunity to soak up the knowledge of the owner, Chris Dyer, who has extensive experience in both archeology and agriculture. At the croft, you can learn about sustainable sheep farming – both theory and practice – and Chris can also arrange guided tours of Bressay and wider Shetland.

Bressay Lighthouse
MAP PAGE 36
Bressay, ZE2 9ER. Free.

At the end of the south road is Bressay Lighthouse, built in the 1850s by David and Thomas Stevenson. The light was removed in 2012 and can now be seen, along with its mechanism, in the Shetland Museum in Lerwick. The former lighthouse keepers' cottages, meanwhile, were self-catering accommodation for several years but are currently not available for booking.

Excellent walks head southwest from the lighthouse along the coast. At the very least, if you take a quick walk out to the small headland almost immediately

The Rescues and Wrecks Trail

While on Bressay, keep your eyes open for information boards telling the stories of the various ships that have been wrecked in these waters over the centuries. The boards are the result of a project by Bressay Primary School, and they contain some fascinating and evocative tales.

next to the lighthouse you'll see a spectacular rock arch behind you, seeming to support the lighthouse. You could continue along this path for several kilometres to the Giant's Leg, or dip inland after about 800 metres and start a climb up to the Ward of Bressay, linking it with the route from Mail for a circular outing.

North to Heogan

MAP PAGE 36
Bressay, ZE2 9EL. Free.
Taking the road that threads up the northwestern coast of Bressay will take you past a couple of minor points of interest. The first of these, almost immediately on your left, is the privately owned Gardie House, an imposing building dating from 1724 which was the former laird's home. About a kilometre on, at a vantage point overlooking Lerwick, the concrete structures on the right are the remains of World War II era anti-aircraft gun stations. Of interest largely only to enthusiasts, taking the short track up to them is nevertheless worth it for the splendid panoramic views. The Cruester Burnt Mound originally stood by the coast in this area, but there's nothing to see at the site now.

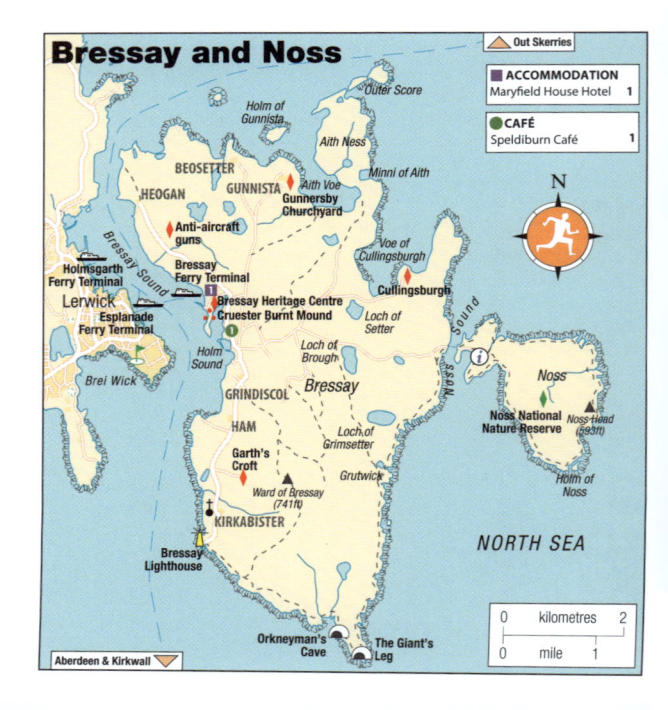

Bressay Lighthouse

Gunnersby Churchyard

MAP PAGE 36
Bressay, ZE2 9EP. Free.

The Gunnersby churchyard, once home to an ancient church but now housing the derelict ruins of an eighteenth-century mausoleum, is a picturesque spot with great views over Aith Voe to Aith Ness opposite.

Aith Ness

MAP PAGE 36
Bressay, ZE2 9EP. Free.

The peninsula of Aith Ness offers an enjoyable walk, which you can begin from a rough track off the road to Setter. The seven-kilometre route takes you past the Loch of Aith and out onto the headland, eventually leading you to a gun dating from World War I. Along the way, you will pass old slate quarries, and are in with a good chance of spotting seals.

Cullingsbrough

MAP PAGE 36
Bressay, ZE2 9ES. Free.

Accessible via a coastal walk from a small parking area at Setter, the site of Cullingsbrough offers scattered remains which span nearly 4000 years. Though there's also a Bronze Age burnt mound and Viking longhouses to seek out, the most prominent of the ruins are in and around the enclosed churchyard, where you'll find the low walls of a twelfth-century church which was built in the shape of a cross, the only one in Shetland to use this architectural style. Nearby is a replica of an eighth-century Pictish carved stone which was found on the site; the original is in Edinburgh's National Museum of Scotland. Meanwhile, just outside the churchyard, you'll find the fairly scant remains of an Iron Age broch.

Loch of Brough

MAP PAGE 36
Bressay, ZE2 9ES. Free.

The Loch of Brough is the start point for walks down the eastern coast, with a track leading from the loch's edge to eventually reach the rugged coastline. It's also the site of a community woodland project, which began in 2022 with

The Giant's Leg

At the southern tip of Bressay is an enormous rock arch, known as the Giant's Leg. It's an extremely impressive formation, which is best seen from the water. Boat trips around Bressay and Noss, originating in Lerwick, usually offer a view of the Leg, and sometimes will head underneath it, if sea conditions are favourable. Recommended operators include Shetland Seabird Tours (http://shetlandseabirdtours.com) and Seabirds and Seals (http://seabirds-and-seals.com).

the planting of trees in a protected area stretching down the loch's western shore.

Grutwick
MAP PAGE 36
Bressay, ZE2 9ES. Free.
If you take the walk south along the eastern coast, you'll reach Grutwick after about three kilometres. Here stands a memorial cairn to William Deacon, who lost his life during the rescue attempt of the crew of the MV *Green Lily*, a ship which ran aground here in 1997.

Noss Sound
MAP PAGE 36
Bressay, ZE2 9ES. Free.
At the end of the island's easternmost road is a car park, from which you can look out over Noss Sound, the narrow channel separating Bressay from the nearby island of Noss. Between May and August you can pick up a ferry which runs on demand across the Sound. Next to the ferry departure point is a grassy mound which is all that remains of an Iron Age broch.

Noss Sound

Gannet colony on the cliffs of Noss

Even if you're not making the trip to Noss, it's worth a stop here: it's a fine wildlife-watching site, with seabirds aplenty, regular seal and porpoise sightings, and the occasional visit from orcas and minke whales. You could also pick up a long path heading south from here, which leads eventually round to the Bressay Lighthouse, or, for a shorter walk, venture out onto Anderhill to make for the early twentieth-century naval watchtower on the summit.

Noss

MAP PAGE 36
Noss, ZE1 0LL. http://nature.scot/enjoying-outdoors/visit-our-nature-reserves/noss-national-nature-reserve. Charge.
Accessed by the small ferry from the eastern side of Bressay, the island of Noss is one of Shetland's – and indeed Scotland's – best places to see seabirds. During the summer months, the island's high cliffs are alive with multiple species – puffins, guillemots, fulmars, gannets and more – while further inland you'll no doubt make the acquaintance of the great skua. Walking around the island's coastline should take you about four hours, offering outstanding wildlife spotting opportunities at almost every turn. As well as watching the birds, remember to keep an eye on the sea: orcas and porpoises are not uncommon.

Café

Speldiburn Café

MAP PAGE 36
Gunnista Rd, Mail, Bressay, ZE2 9EN. http://facebook.com/speldiburncafe.
Housed in the former primary school, Speldiburn Café is the perfect spot for lunch while you're on Bressay, offering paninis, sandwiches and soup, as well as a tempting array of cakes. There's a small craft shop here too, and a room which sometimes has exhibitions of local interest topics. £

South Mainland

Head south from Lerwick and you'll reach some of Shetland's top sights: it's here that you'll find archeological wonders such as Jarlshof and the Broch of Mousa, as well as the iconic double-sided beach of St Ninian's Isle. There are also stunning coastal walks to be had in the area – try the circuit around Fladdabister, or the out-and-back route to the Ness of Burgi – and, above all, outstanding wildlife spotting opportunities, most notably from the Mainland's southernmost point at Sumburgh Head. All in all, this is a part of Shetland that's well worth exploring in depth: allow yourself three days at the least.

Gulberwick

MAP PAGE 42
Off A970, Gulberwick, ZE2 9JX. Free.

The small village of Gulberwick, just south of Lerwick, overlooks a pretty little bay, which can be accessed by a track starting just down from the church. The beach is both pebbly and sandy, and is a pleasant spot on a warm day. A path leads from here back round the coast to Lerwick, which makes for an easy coastal ramble.

Just outside Gulberwick, on the main A970 road, you'll see what appears to be a standing stone on top of a scree bank. This is not in fact a Neolithic survivor, but instead a slightly unexpected monument to the Shetland Road Reconstruction Programme of 1980. It is not worth the awkward scramble to get up to it.

Fladdabister

MAP PAGE 42
Off A970, Fladdabister, ZE2 9HA. Free.

View fom St Ninian's Isle

A walk around Fladdabister

An enjoyable walking circuit of about two hours begins from the road heading down to the village of Fladdabister. From the sign marked 'Access Route', head through the gate and, ignoring the obvious track to the left, head to the right towards the wind turbine. Follow the path across the field as it bends left past some rocky crags, and descends, sometimes steeply, with a wall and fence on your right and coastal views gradually opening up ahead of you. As the fence bends right, follow it, but cross over to the left-hand side of the small stream that joins you here, and continue until you reach the low cliffs.

Admire the lovely view for a while, then turn left and follow the coastline. If it's nesting season, keep inland a bit here to avoid disturbing the seabirds, but ideally you'll be able to stick to the cliff edge because there's some stunning coastal scenery here to admire, including a row of five gorgeous sea caves.

After rounding the bay with the caves, you'll soon descend to the pretty Mill Burn. Turn left and follow its course past numerous attractive little cascades. It soon becomes a narrow channel, cutting its way through the earth; keep following it on its left side until you see a clutch of ruined farm cottages. Here the path crosses the burn and you climb towards the picturesque ruins.

Keep the ruins on your left, and after passing the last one, stay with the path as it heads towards a stone bridge, at which you should cross the burn and follow the line of stones, then, when they peter out, keep going in the same general direction. From this point on the path is unfortunately very indistinct; you'll keep coming across it but losing it again. To keep your bearings, you'll ascend a small rise, from the top of which you can see a large grey farm building – try to keep this directly ahead of you.

From the top of the rise, the Loch of Fladdabister will come into view. Descend towards it, and when you reach the shore, turn left. Skirt along the water's edge, using the path which is mostly visible at this stage. Keep with the loch as it bends right until you reach a line of fence posts, at which point it's time to cut inland and make for the grey farm building ahead, sometimes with the path but more often without. Eventually, you'll hit a wide vehicle track: turn left and follow it back to the walk's start point.

Fladdabister is a small village that straggles along the coast just below the A970. A farming community for hundreds of years, it has now added a smattering of good B&Bs to its local economy. The small bay beneath the village offers a pebbly beach, accessed by a pleasant tramp across grassy fields and past the ruins of nineteenth-century lime kilns, which were once big business in the area. From the beach, if you're in the mood for a longer walk, you could follow the path along the coast past the Bay of Okraquoy to the village of Aith.

Aith Voe Harbour
MAP PAGE 42
Off A970, Cunningsburgh, ZE2 9HF. Free.
This pretty little fishing harbour is worth a quick stop if you're nearby in August or September. Thanks to the easy access to fresh fish, seals can often be spotted here at extremely close range, particularly

South Mainland

SHOPS
Karlin Anderson	2
Nielanell	1

ACCOMMODATION
Ben End B&B	1
Hayhoull B&B	2
Sumburgh Hotel	4
Sumburgh Lighthouse	5
Voortrekker Shetland	3

RESTAURANTS AND CAFÉS
Hoswick Visitor Centre	1
Sumburgh Head Observatory	3
Sumburgh Hotel	2

Cunningsburgh
MAP PAGE 42
Off A970, Cunningsburgh, ZE2 9HF. Free.

There's a little sandy beach at Cunningsburgh, which is attractive enough but is overlooked by the A970 and is therefore not particularly peaceful. More tranquil, perhaps, is the view from the Cunningsburgh cemetery, just a couple of hundred metres eastward. From here, you can gaze out over a glassy bay, dotted with small rocks on which shags perch, with the island of Mousa offering a perfect backdrop.

Catpund
MAP PAGE 42
A970, ZE3 9JW. Free.

There's little left to see of the former Norse site of Catpund, which isn't very easy to find. To track it down, take the track up from the layby on the A970 just south of Cunningsburgh, and when you reach the remains of an ancient quarry, you'll see a stile to your left. Cross this and head over to the burn, where the ruins of buildings will come into view. If you head upstream here, you'll find an info board, which explains that the Vikings quarried this hillside for steatite – or soapstone – from which they made objects such as bowls, lamps and other household items. Even without checking out the remains, a stop here is worthwhile: the view across the bay from this vantage point is beautiful.

Leebitton Mousa Museum
MAP PAGE 42
Sandsayre Pier, Leebitton, ZE2 9HP. Free.

While waiting for the boat to Mousa, step into the small Leebitton Mousa Museum on the quayside and explore the history of Leebitton village and the island opposite. The museum's centrepiece is a flitboat, a large green rowing boat which was the only regular transport to Mousa until well into the twentieth century. Around the flitboat are numerous other artefacts of life in Leebitton: lifebelts, a herring scoop, even a Russian buoy found in the waters here. As well as the exhibits, there are multiple information boards on topics ranging from the Broch of Mousa to the copper mining operations in nearby Sandlodge.

Mousa
MAP PAGE 42
Ferry from Sandsayre Pier, Leebitton, ZE2 9HP. http://rspb.org.uk/days-out/reserves/mousa. Charge.

The island of Mousa sits a ten-minute ferry ride from the village of Leebitton, and makes for a perfect excursion, offering splendid opportunities for spotting seabirds as well as being home to Scotland's best-preserved Iron Age broch. The island is an RSPB reserve and access is by ferry only; these run at 11.30am daily except Saturdays between April and September, and

Mousa Ferry

Broch and roll

Brochs are unique to Scotland: they can be found all over the country, though there's a particular concentration in the far northeast, including Orkney and Shetland. Constructed in the Iron Age, their purpose remains unclear: one theory suggests that they were defensive structures, but archeologists since the 1980s have tended to consider that brochs were in fact intended as a display of wealth and status, akin to a stately home.

---

give you slightly less than three hours to explore the island. Pre-booking is not possible, and the ferry is a cash-only service.

The northern end of the island is out of bounds, but a well-marked path leads around the southern section. It's a circular route which will take you about two hours to cover.

The first point of interest is East Ham, a pretty little bay with a stony beach, often a popular hangout for shags and seals. Follow the path as it climbs to the top of the bay, and enjoy lovely views of the sea crashing against the rocks. From here, the path leads around to the rocky shore of the eastern side of the island. These cliffs are nesting sites for numerous seabirds, including Arctic skuas, which may become aggressive if you get too close during nesting season – heed the signs and stick to the path.

Passing a drystone wall, a couple of smaller islands just off Mousa now come into view. The largest of these, Peerie Bard, has a small lighthouse on it. As the path gets closer to it, you'll enjoy ever better views of the sea battering the jagged rocks.

Descending along the line of a drystone wall, you'll arrive at East Pool, a good place to spot seals if you linger a while. The nearby West Pool, which grandly proclaims itself to be Selkie Kingdom, is similarly good for seal-spotting, and is also home to Arctic terns and Arctic skuas. To keep this wealth of wildlife safe, ensure you stay on the path.

Ahead of you, you'll see the ruins of old cottages, built in the eighteenth century for former crofters, while in the distance you'll also be able to spot the Broch of Mousa, to which you're now headed. As you approach, on the left you can see the remains of the large house where the island's owner lived in the nineteenth century.

At an impressive 13 metres high, towering over the shoreline of the island, the Broch of Mousa is the best preserved of all Scotland's brochs. Entering through its low doorway, you can admire the thickness of its walls and the effort which went into its construction.

The Broch of Mousa

It can be climbed via an internal staircase, giving you access to great views from the top. The broch is sometimes kept locked, but even then, you can take a look through the bars of the door to get an idea of the interior.

Once you've admired the broch, continue along the path past the stony beach, keeping an eye open for the seals that frequent the water here. Thereafter, ascend the grassy path onto the cliffs, passing a rock favoured by shags, and glancing back for fine views of the broch. Before long, you'll arrive back at the pier.

Sandwick Beach
MAP PAGE 42
Sandwick, ZE2 9HW. Free.

The beach at Sandwick lives up to its name: it's sandy, and has calm water which is ideal for a paddle on a warm day. It's found just beneath the village's well-kept church, where there's a handy car park if you're planning on walking to the Broch of Burraland.

The Broch of Burraland
MAP PAGE 42
Sandwick, ZE2 9HW. Free.

Judging by its diameter, the Broch of Burraland was probably as impressive in its day as the Broch of Mousa, visible just across the water. No doubt vessels passing through the Mousa Sound, with these two imposing brochs flanking each shore, would have been reminded of the power of the local chieftains.

Today, Burraland's broch is largely ruined, though the walls are still around two metres high in parts, and it's possible to see remnants of the double-skinning wall construction technique. There are further ruins and visible foundations close by on the headland, suggesting that the site was more than just the broch. It's in a stunning location, with expansive views in every direction, and is well worth the walk to get here.

Sandwick

Access isn't as obvious as you might hope: there are no signs pointing the way, and there's nowhere to park nearer than the church at Sandwick, from which it's a roughly 30-minute walk up a road signposted to The Wart and then veering up a farm track on the left. About ten minutes along this, don't enter the field which seems to offer a direct route toward the broch; instead, keep right and follow the fence to the coast, where you climb over a stile and head left past beautiful rugged cliffs. Alternative, longer routes exist along the coastal path from Leebitton, or you can walk the entire Noness peninsula.

Noness
MAP PAGE 42
Sandwick, ZE2 9HW. Free.

The Noness peninsula is an excellent choice for a circular coastal walk. Starting from the Sandwick church car park, the route is about seven kilometres in length, and includes a visit to the Broch of Burraland as well as ample opportunities to spot seabirds. It's

St Ninian

St Ninian, the patron saint of Shetland, is traditionally held to have been an early Christian missionary who converted the southern Picts and established a church at Whithorn, Galloway, in the early fifth century. Missionaries from this church may have subsequently visited Orkney and Shetland spreading Christianity, and it is thought that the church on St Ninian's Isle was modelled on the Whithorn original.

easy to follow, as you're essentially just walking along the cliffs. The full route goes all the way to Leebitton and then follows the road back to Sandwich, but you could cut it short by taking the farm track back from the broch.

Hoswick Visitor Centre
MAP PAGE 42
Hoswick, ZE2 9HL.
http://hoswickvisitorcentre.com. Free.
The visitor centre at Hoswick makes a very worthy stop: as well as the excellent café (see page 51) and the well-stocked gift shop, there's also an interesting exhibition on various topics of local interest, including the history of the whaling industry, information on the Broch of Burraland, and a display of tweeds made in the village. Across the road in the car park, there are further information boards: don't miss the reproduction of the fascinating 1907 newspaper article detailing the first ever car to visit Hoswick.

Hoswick Beach
MAP PAGE 42
Hoswick, ZE2 9HL. Free.
Hoswick's pretty little beach is mostly shingle, though there's a small expanse of sand too. The water is clean and clear, and though it's rarely warm, it can be tempting to take a brief dip. For those who prefer to stay dry, there's a path running south from the beach offering a pleasant coastal stroll.

Levenwick Beach
MAP PAGE 42
Levenwick, ZE2 9HX. Free.
Nestled in a calm bay on the eastern coast a few kilometres south of Hoswick, the village of Levenwick is home to a very pleasant yellow sand beach, which is perfect for taking a dip if you happen to catch it on a warm – or at least sunny – day. Otherwise, it's still a lovely spot for an easy stroll along the sand.

St Ninian's Isle
MAP PAGE 42
Bigton, ZE2 9JA. Free.
One of Shetland's most iconic natural wonders, St Ninian's Isle is connected to Mainland by a wide sandbar known as a tombolo, which essentially makes it a double-sided beach, washed by the waves from both north and south. You can walk across it onto the island, which has a couple of minor archeological sites, including St Ninian's Chapel, famed for the discovery in 1958 of a hoard of silver treasure dating from the eighth or ninth century, now on show in Lerwick's Shetland Museum. Alternatively, you can make use of the beach's Haar Sauna, warming yourself up before making a dash for a cold plunge in the sea.

Rerwick Beach
MAP PAGE 42
B9122, ZE2 9JF. Free.
A fine sandy cove which is very popular with seals, Rerwick Beach can be viewed from several passing places on the road above but, given the seal population, it's best not to

venture onto the beach itself as you may disturb them.

Spiggie Loch
MAP PAGE 42
Spiggie Lane, off B9122, ZE2 9JE. Free.
Spiggie Loch is a renowned spot for birdwatching and trout fishing, so bring your binoculars or rod. There's an RSPB hide for twitching even in unpleasant weather, opposite which is an access road for Scousburgh Sands, a wide and sheltered bay, with fine white sand and attractive views across to Rerwick.

Shetland Crofthouse Museum
MAP PAGE 42
Boddam Way, off A970, ZE2 9JG. http://shetlandmuseumandarchives.org.uk/visit/crofthouse-museum. Free, donations welcome.

This original crofthouse, built in 1850, remained in use as a farm until the 1960s. It's in a perfect state of preservation, still with its thick stone walls and thatched roof, complete with low doorways, uneven floors, and a warming smoky peat fire. There is all manner of period-appropriate furniture throughout, with box beds, cradles, spinning wheels, a lovely clock on the mantelpiece and a fiddle hanging on the wall. It's an essential stop to get an insight into the way of life for crofters in the nineteenth and early twentieth centuries.

Quendale Mill
MAP PAGE 42
Quendale Ln, Dunrossness, ZE2 9JD. http://quendalemill.co.uk. Charge.
The mid-nineteenth century mill at Quendale, used until the 1970s, has been lovingly restored and is now open as a museum, which you can explore to learn the process by which the mill operated. There's a self-guided tour through the mill's multiple rooms, which starts with a video introduction and then moves into the threshing rooms, the kilns and to the grain chutes. As well as the mill's equipment, such as sack hoists and meal sieves, there are excellent displays on other subjects of local interest, including a room on the oil spillage disaster in 1993 when the tanker *Braer* ran aground in the waters nearby. There's a motley collection of other items too: a large display of worldwide currency, some toy lorries and buses, and pieces of debris from the White Star Line ship *Oceanic*, which was wrecked off Foula in 1914. Finally, don't miss the mill's

Shetland Crofthouse Museum

fine waterwheel, on the outside of the building.

The mill has a handy little tourist information point and a good gift shop, where you'll find a fine range of Shetland souvenirs, particularly knitwear.

Old Scatness Broch and Iron Age Village

MAP PAGE 42
A970, Scatness, Sumburgh, ZE3 9JW. http://shetlandamenity.org/old-scatness. Charge.

Just south of Sumburgh Airport are the substantial remains of an Iron Age village, discovered in 1975 when road construction works revealed the edge of the broch. Excavations are ongoing, but you can see numerous building – including several wheelhouses, a construction unique to Scotland – arranged around the central broch. The site has yielded several amazing finds, including a Pictish carving of a bear which is now on display in Lerwick's Shetland Museum. The site is only open in summer, and even then sporadically, so check the website if you want to arrange a visit.

Ness of Burgi

MAP PAGE 42
Off A970, Sumburgh, ZE3 9JT. Free.

The Ness of Burgi, a headland opposite Sumburgh Head, is a picturesque spot worth the twenty-minute ramble to its tip, where you'll find an Iron Age fort known as a blockhouse. The walk starts from a turning area at the end of the Scatness road; there is room to park here, but space is limited, so make sure to park considerately. Pass through the gate and then take the easy path heading south towards the end of the peninsula. The headland gradually gets more rugged until it narrows to a rocky ledge a couple of metres wide – cross this with the aid of the handrail.

Once across, the blockhouse is on a promontory ahead and slightly left. This rectangular building has several rooms into which you could crawl if you're so inclined and a huge lintel over the main doorway. Its function is unknown, but it seems to date from roughly the same time as Shetland's brochs.

Jarlshof archeological site

West Voe Beach
MAP PAGE 42
A970, Sumburgh, ZE3 9JD. Free.
This sandy little beach sits just south of Sumburgh Airport, making it a fun place to paddle in the sea while planes fly disconcertingly close. Like many places on this southern tip of Shetland, it's archeologically significant: finds here suggest human habitation from as long as 6500 years ago.

Jarlshof
MAP PAGE 42
Off A970, Sumburgh, ZE3 9JN.
http://historicenvironment.scot/visit-a-place/places/jarlshof-prehistoric-and-norse-settlement. Charge.
The archeological site of Jarlshof was inhabited from around 2500 BC until the 1600s, and there are ruins here from almost every point in between, from Bronze Age chambered houses through to the seventeenth-century manor. The site was unknown until the 1890s, when it was uncovered by a heavy storm, and excavations were undertaken from the 1930s onwards. Many of the ruins can be entered and explored, allowing a very interactive visit. The free audio guides are informative and engaging, so it's worth picking one up.

The Visitor Centre contains plenty of information, giving details on all the different styles of building you'll see here, including a 3D display which helps you to understand from which era the various constructions date. There are a few artefacts from the site on display too, but most findings are either in the Shetland Museum in Lerwick or in Edinburgh's National Museum of Scotland.

Leaving the Visitor Centre, at the end of the path to your right you'll find the remains of the earliest houses yet discovered at Jarlshof. These trace foundations indicate the size and shape of the dwellings in around 2000 BC. Back toward the Visitor Centre are later houses, from around 800 BC, now set into the earth but their low stone walls and multiple chambers plain to see. One building from this era, thought to have been a smithy, is paved, allowing you to enter it and explore the rooms and workshops. Many impressive bronze-worked artefacts have been recovered from Jarlshof.

Follow the path round, past further Bronze Age dwellings – look out for the quern, for grain grinding, in the house just as you round the corner to the right. Now walking alongside the sea, you'll pass more Bronze Age houses before you reach the remains of the site's broch, which dates to around 400 BC. Though only one half now remains, it's clear from the width of the semicircle that it was originally a building of considerable size. Brochs were built with two walls, an inner and an outer, allowing them to reach a greater height while keeping the use of stone to a minimum. The alcoves in the wall allow you to get a good look at how this was achieved.

Brochs are uniquely Scottish, and the path now leads you to another example of architecture only found in Scotland – the wheelhouse. There are two wheelhouses at Jarlshof: they're both fascinating, but the more complete one is the second, found after you follow the path on a bend round to the right. These structures take their name from their resemblance to a wheel, with rooms like spokes coming off a central hub, which was likely where the hearth was. Inside, the separate rooms are still perfectly preserved, with stone and turf roofs, and on a windy day, you can really appreciate how snug these houses would have been.

Opposite the wheelhouse are the foundations of Viking longhouses, one of them truly earning the name

Sumburgh Head Lighthouse

Sumburgh Head

MAP PAGE 42
Sumburgh Head Ln, Sumburgh, ZE3 9JN.
http://sumburghhead.com. Charge.

Sumburgh Head, the southernmost point on Mainland, is a promontory topped by a lighthouse and museum. On the walk up, keep your eyes peeled for marine life: this is an excellent place to spot a wide range of seabirds, plus dolphins and whales. There's a sheltered lookout point along the route, as well as a large model of an orca which serves as minor consolation if you haven't seen the real thing.

The museum consists of numerous rooms across several buildings. Just next to the ticket desk is a room containing the machinery for operating the foghorn, as well as information on the construction and history of the lighthouse and foghorn. The lighthouse was designed in 1812 by Robert Stevenson, a prolific lighthouse architect and grandfather of the *Treasure Island* author Robert Louis Stevenson. The foghorn, meanwhile, was in operation from 1864, and is no longer used except to signal the beginning and end of the tourist season.

Next door, in the smiddy, you'll find fascinating biographical information about several of the lighthouse keepers who worked at Sumburgh Head, while opposite is an excellent exhibition on local marine life, including displays on killer whales and auks. Exiting the marine exhibition will bring you to the foot of the lighthouse itself, beyond which is a smaller radar hut detailing the important role Sumburgh Head played in foiling a German raid on Scapa Flow in Orkney during World War II.

Last but not least, there's an observatory with enormous glass windows, offering views looking north back up towards Jarlshof. Here you'll find an honesty box system for tea, coffee and cakes.

'long'. The Vikings seem to have settled here in the ninth century AD, and remained at Jarlshof for several centuries. Plenty of Viking artefacts have been found here, giving considerable insight into their way of life. From the longhouse, it was a simple step of architectural evolution to the larger medieval farmhouse, which sits alongside it.

Finally, you'll reach the largest and most recent building on site: the laird's house. This sizeable residence was home to the steward who oversaw Shetland on behalf of the Earls of Orkney. The name of the entire site, Jarlshof ('Earl's house'), is taken from this building, courtesy of the novelist Walter Scott. There's a viewing platform at the top of the remains of the great hall, from which you can survey much of the site.

After leaving, from the Visitor Centre you can pick up a path that takes you along the coast to Sumburgh Head. It's a very picturesque walk, but it involves some ascent, so be prepared to climb a bit.

Shops

Karlin Anderson
MAP PAGE 42
The Beach Road Workshop, Hoswick, ZE2 9HL. http://karlinanderson.com.
If you're on the lookout for unique jewellery, this little shop by Hoswick Beach is the place to come. Bespoke pieces can be made to order in the onsite workshop, or you can choose from Karlin's existing ranges, which take inspiration from Shetland culture and Norse mythology, among other themes.

Nielanell
MAP PAGE 42
Hoswick Rd, Hoswick, ZE2 9HL. http://nielanell.com.
Forget any ideas about staid and stolid cardigans: Nielanell brings a real sense of innovation to traditional Shetland knitwear. The pieces on sale in this shop are bold and striking, with eye-catching choices of colour. It's not cheap, but it is individual.

Restaurant

Sumburgh Hotel
MAP PAGE 42
Sumburgh, ZE3 9JN. http://sumburghhotel.com/eat.
The dining room of the Sumburgh Hotel is open to non-residents, though it's advisable to book in advance. The extensive menu runs to various classic pub meals, with burgers, fish and chips, scampi and curries all making an appearance, with a couple of wild cards thrown in such as stir-fried sweet chilli duck with rice. ££

Cafés

Hoswick Visitor Centre
MAP PAGE 42
Hoswick, ZE2 9HL. http://hoswickvisitorcentre.com.
Hoswick's visitor centre has a very welcome café, which serves up coffee, cakes, and excellent breakfasts and lunches. The Voe Bannock – a Shetland bread cake with salt beef – is a very good choice, but there are also options including quiches, mackerel pâté and hummus, as well as plenty of sandwiches and paninis. £

Sumburgh Head Observatory
MAP PAGE 42
Sumburgh Head Ln, Sumburgh, ZE3 9JN. http://sumburghhead.com.
If you're looking for a place to spot seabirds and marine life while you drink a cup of coffee, you've found the right place – the enormous windows in the Sumburgh Head Observatory offer fantastic panoramas, and there's an honesty box system for coffee and cakes. £

Sumburgh Head Observatory

Fair Isle

There's something quite special about making a trip to Fair Isle, which is by some considerable distance Shetland's remotest island. Sitting in the middle of the North Sea, halfway between Shetland and Orkney, it's well known for its iconic knitwear and is also a marvellous destination for birdwatchers, its position making it an ideal stop for migratory species rarely seen elsewhere in the UK. Add to that some splendid coastal scenery which makes perfect walking country, and it's easy to see why it's well worth making a visit to this remote outpost.

North Haven

MAP PAGE 52
Fair Isle, ZE2 9JU. Free.

If arriving by ferry, you'll make landfall on Fair Isle in North Haven, a pretty little sheltered harbour which boasts an attractive sandy beach. Seals can often be seen here, and the beach makes a pleasant spot for a chilly dip. To the east of the harbour is the Buness peninsula, offering an easy coastal walk with some gorgeous scenery.

Fair Isle Observatory

MAP PAGE 52

Getting to Fair Isle

Fair Isle can be reached by both air and sea. Flights, which leave from Tingwall Airport, take 25 minutes, and depart at least once a day (except Sundays) during the summer months. On most days there are multiple flights, opening up the chance to make a day trip: check the current timetable at http://airtask.com/passenger-transport. Bookings must be made by phone (01595 840246) or email (lwk.ops@airtask.com). If you're coming from Orkney, in summer Loganair (http://loganair.co.uk) offers a twice-weekly flight from Kirkwall.

If you prefer to travel by sea, ferries can be picked up from Grutness near Sumburgh. In summer, there are three sailings a week, and just one in winter. It takes 2hr 30 min, and it's worth bearing in mind that the crossing can be quite rough. The ferry carries foot passengers only, not cars, though work began in April 2024 to build a new car ferry terminal on Fair Isle; it's expected to be in operation by spring 2026. Given the infrequent sailing times, it's not possible to do a day trip to Fair Isle by ferry.

Fair Isle, ZE2 9JU.
http://fairislebirdobs.co.uk. Free.
Fair Isle is an outstanding place for birdwatchers, as it's home to large colonies of seabirds as well as being an important stopover point for migratory land birds: many species more usually found in Siberia or Eastern Asia can be found here with a degree of regularity. Recognising the island's importance for birds, an observatory was built here in 1948 by George Waterston, a keen ornithologist who owned Fair Isle between 1947 and 1954. Until a fire destroyed the observatory in 2019, it provided accommodation and meals for visitors. Rebuilding is underway, with the observatory expected to fully reopen in 2025; in the meantime, the observatory still offers ranger-guided trips around the island to spot birds and wildlife. Leaflets on self-guided expeditions can also be found here.

Landberg
MAP PAGE 52
Fair Isle, ZE2 9JU. Free.
Fair Isle isn't particularly rich in archeological remains, offering only a couple of sites of minor interest. Landberg is one of them: although there's little to see, it's thought that this promontory just south of the observatory was once used as a fort, possibly during the early medieval period. Low ramparts can still be made out, but in honesty, although the setting is pretty, the remains are for enthusiasts only.

North Haven

Fair Isle knitwear

Worn by everyone from Edward VIII and Paul McCartney to Monty Python's Gumbys, Fair Isle knitwear is famous around the world. The technique, which appears to have originated in the eighteenth century, involves using two colours per round, often producing relatively simple geometric shapes or motifs known as the OXO pattern – essentially, a row of O shapes connected by X shapes. The overall effect can be quite complex, especially if additional colours are incorporated on subsequent rounds, producing bright and often striking jumpers, hats and scarves. There's a good display of Fair Isle knitwear in the island's George Waterston Museum, as well as in the Shetland Museum in Lerwick.

North Lighthouse

MAP PAGE 52
Fair Isle, ZE2 9JU. http://nlb.org.uk/lighthouses/fair-isle-north-skroo. Free.
Fair Isle's northernmost point is crowned by a lighthouse standing proudly at the top of 65m-tall cliffs. Built in the 1890s by the ever-busy Stevensons, it was automated in 1983 and the keeper's cottage was demolished. It's a good starting point for walks along the northern coast to the Stacks of Skroo, a set of impressive rock features off Fair Isle's northwest corner.

North Lighthouse

Ward Hill

MAP PAGE 52
Fair Isle, ZE2 9JU. Free.
Ward Hill, an easy climb from just north of the island's airstrip, is Fair Isle's highest point, at 217 metres high. The summit is marked by a trig point, and on a clear day it offers fantastic views: you may be able to see all the way to Sumburgh Head on Shetland's Mainland, or to the Orkney island of North Ronaldsay. If you descend the hill to the west, you could extend the walk with a stroll along the rugged coastline before looping back inland to return to the airstrip.

Sheep Rock

MAP PAGE 52
Fair Isle, ZE2 9JU. Free.
On the east coast, a little way south of the observatory, is the easily recognisable Sheep Rock, a promontory connected to Fair Isle by a narrow neck of rock. Although some enthusiastic sheep sometimes manage to clamber onto it – hence the name – it's best admired from the safety of the cliffs.

Vaasetter

MAP PAGE 52
Fair Isle, ZE2 9JU. Free.
Roughly in the centre of the island, the small settlement of Vaasetter is home to remnants of two vastly different periods in Fair Isle's history. Firstly, in the fields nearby

El Gran Grifón

Perhaps the most famous Fair Isle shipwreck is *El Gran Grifón*, one of the flagships of the Spanish Armada in 1588. Having been defeated in the English Channel, *El Gran Grifón* had escaped into the North Sea and – having located other surviving Spanish ships – the crew were attempting to make their way home around Scotland. They had almost reached Ireland, but were thrown northwards by a strong storm, and were forced to attempt to land on Fair Isle to effect repairs. Unfortunately, adverse tides resulted in the ship foundering on the rocks of Stroms Hellier, on the eastern coast. The crew were able to get ashore safely, and seem to have been welcomed by the locals. Even so, many of the survivors subsequently died on Fair Isle from previously sustained wounds, and are now buried in the cemetery at South Harbour.

you'll be able to find the eastern end of the Feely Dyke, the ancient earthwork which divided the island in two; and secondly, by the side of the road here is the wreck of a German Heinkel plane, which crashed here in 1941.

George Waterston Museum
MAP PAGE 52
Fair Isle, ZE2 9JU. 01595 760244. Free.
Housed in the island's former school, this museum is home to exhibitions on many aspects of Fair Isle's history and culture, with a particular focus on its famous knitwear. There's also plenty of information about local birdlife, the island's wartime experiences, and the many ships that have been wrecked on its shores.

Malcolm's Head
MAP PAGE 52
Fair Isle, ZE2 9JU. Free.
An easy circular walk starts from the George Waterston Museum and heads out to the magnificent coastal scenery of Malcolm's Head, which boasts cliffs more than one hundred metres high. The route heads along the cliff edge, offering fantastic views of rock arches and rugged coastline, as well as the opportunity to see large numbers of seabirds during the nesting season. Allow up to two hours for the walk.

South Lighthouse
MAP PAGE 52
Fair Isle, ZE2 9JU. http://nlb.org.uk/lighthouses/fair-isle-south. Free.
This was the last lighthouse in Scotland to be automated, with the keepers remaining until 1998. Like the North Lighthouse, it was built by the Stevensons in 1892, and its most notable hour was perhaps in 1941, when it was damaged by a German air raid. In response, the island's Principal Keeper, Roderick Macaulay, walked three miles through snow and wind to help repair the lighthouse, then the same distance back to take his regular shift at the North Lighthouse.

Eating and drinking

There are no cafés or restaurants on Fair Isle at time of writing, although when the observatory reopens it may be possible to get a meal there. In the meantime, to get provisions, you'll need to either bring food with you, or stop off at Stackhoull Stores, the island's only shop, at the settlement of Stonybreck.

Central Mainland

West of Lerwick, the Central Mainland encompasses the historic villages of Tingwall, home to Shetland's parliament in the Norse era, and Scalloway, which until the early eighteenth century was Shetland's capital. Stretching south from Scalloway, and connected to Mainland by bridges, are the three islands of Trondra, West Burra and East Burra, which offer some lovely beaches and attractive walking country. To the region's north, meanwhile, you'll find Whiteness and Weisdale, which can be taken in on a marvellously scenic drive towards Westside.

Tingwall
MAP PAGE 58
Tingwall, ZE2 9SD. Free.

Tingwall is a fairly spread out settlement, with houses stretching from the central area of Veensgarth all the way along the edge of Strand Loch, which is a pretty body of water overlooked by gentle hills. It gives out into the sea at its northern end, with peninsulas stretching along both sides: a gentle walk follows the water's edge on the western side from Laxfirth, which can be extended to the settlement of Wadbister if you want to walk the whole peninsula. Wadbister itself is a small community with lovely views across to the Gletness peninsula opposite.

Law Ting Holm
MAP PAGE 58
B9074, Tingwall, ZE2 9SB. Free.

To the south of Veensgarth is Tingwall Loch, at the north end of which is a spit of land. In centuries gone by, this was an island, and it is here that until around 1600 Shetland's parliament – known as

Scalloway

Earl Patrick Stewart

The rule of Patrick Stewart, the Earl of Orkney from 1593 until 1615, was characterised by arrogance, cruelty and financial irresponsibility, and his various extravagant enterprises – including the building of Scalloway Castle – left him deep in debt. By 1610, complaints against his tyrannical rule by the islanders of both Orkney and Shetland had resulted in his imprisonment in Edinburgh Castle; he was released after giving a promise that he would not try to escape, but he was apparently unable to make it so, as he was subsequently rearrested. His next move was to order his son Robert to engage in rebellion against the crown, with the result that both he and Robert were executed for treason in 1615. Legend has it that Patrick's execution was delayed for several days to allow him time to learn the Lord's Prayer, as he was so evil-hearted that he did not know it.

the lawthing – met to determine laws and hold trials. The name Tingwall has the same Norse root as Tingvellr, the Icelandic location famous for being the site of the world's first parliament.

Asta Golf Club
MAP PAGE 58
B9074, Asta, ZE1 0UQ.
http://astagolfcourse.com. Charge.
In a pretty spot just south of Tingwall Loch, the Asta Golf Club is open to non-members and offers an enjoyable nine-hole course. You're in with a good chance of seeing some local birdlife while you play, with oystercatchers and Arctic terns often seen on the course. Perhaps Asta's most notable feature, though, is the Murder Stone, a standing stone right next to the road on the edge of the course. Apparently, this was the spot on which Henry Sinclair, Earl of Orkney, murdered his cousin and rival Malise Sperra after a rather heated discussion.

Carol's Ponies
MAP PAGE 58
B9074, Asta, ZE1 0UQ. 07990 875845. Free, donations to cancer charity welcome.
For a chance to meet the famous Shetland ponies up close and personal, get in touch with Carol, who has a large herd of them, and can deliver an informative and entertaining introduction to the history and maintenance of the breed. The good-natured ponies can be stroked and sometimes fed. Call in advance to arrange a suitable time for your visit.

Scalloway
MAP PAGE 60
Scalloway, ZE1 0XB. Free.
The village of Scalloway, which dates back at least as far as the Norse period, was Shetland's capital until 1708, and is now most famous as the headquarters of the World War II Shetland Bus operation (see box). It's an attractive place with amenities including shops, hotels and a pub, making it an appealing alternative to Lerwick if you're looking for a place to base yourself for a couple of days.

Scalloway Castle
MAP PAGE 60
Castle St, Scalloway, ZE1 0TQ.
http://historicenvironment.scot/visit-a-place/places/scalloway-castle. Free.
Scalloway's tall and imposing castle dates from the early seventeenth century, built with forced labour on the orders of the notorious Earl of Orkney, Patrick Stewart.

Central Mainland

ACCOMMODATION	
Ervhouse B&B	1
Glen B&B	3
Herrislea House Hotel	2

SHOP	
Burra Bears	1

The Shetland Bus

The Shetland Bus was a top secret operation conducted during World War II, based initially at Lunna but moving to Scalloway in 1942. The project's aim was to support the resistance movement in Nazi-occupied Norway, using Norwegian fishing boats as cover for smuggling secret agents in and rescuing refugees. The Shetland Bus also delivered weaponry to the Norwegian resistance, laid mines and even made an attempt to sink the *Tirpitz*, the Germans' largest battleship. The Shetland Bus operations were crewed by brave people, both military and volunteers, for many of whom the missions ended in tragedy: boats were lost at sea, agents were captured and executed, and several operatives only survived against the odds. Missions continued until 1945, when Norway was liberated.

It had four storeys, with the Great Hall occupying the first floor, and the Earl's private quarters on the floors above. The floors have now collapsed, leaving much of the interior open to the elements. The castle has been closed for renovation since 2020, and at time of writing has no expected reopening date.

Scalloway Museum
MAP PAGE 60
Castle St, Scalloway, ZE1 0TP.
http://scallowaymuseum.org. Charge.
The excellent Scalloway Museum has a fine collection of local interest exhibits, presented in an engaging and modern display. You can explore early twentieth-century fashion, the manufacture of Shetland knitwear, the fishing and whaling industry, and artefacts from the Norse era. There's also a collection of debris salvaged from the White Star Line ship *Oceanic*, wrecked off Foula in 1914. Other displays of interest cover the darker topics of Earl Patrick Stewart's tyranny and the witchcraft trials of the seventeenth century.

The most vital section, though, is the extensive exhibition covering the Shetland Bus project, which was based in Scalloway and operated throughout World War II, supporting the Norwegian resistance movement and saving many lives. The exhibition does a fine job in bringing the personalities of the brave operatives to life, as well as giving a fantastic overview of the whole scheme. The gift shop has a good range of books further exploring Shetland's wartime history.

New Street
MAP PAGE 60
New St, Scalloway, ZE1 0TP. Free.
From the castle, walk to the seafront to take a look at the harbour, which has been a busy place of industry for centuries, then

Scalloway Museum

Scalloway

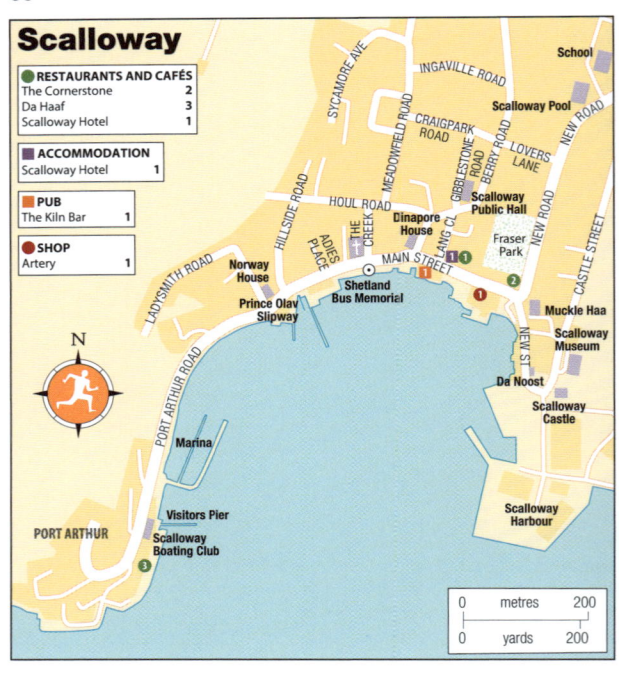

RESTAURANTS AND CAFÉS
The Cornerstone	2
Da Haaf	3
Scalloway Hotel	1

ACCOMMODATION
Scalloway Hotel	1

PUB
The Kiln Bar	1

SHOP
Artery	1

swing round to follow New Street into the town centre. On your right you'll see a row of cottages painted in an array of bright colours, to the right of which is a tiny house called Da Noost. Take a look at the rather opinionated plaque on the wall, inserted by a former owner named William Johnson, who was in fierce disagreement with a group of German scientists about the cause of tides. At the end of the road, above the roundabout, is a large grey building known as the Muckle Haa: it was built in the eighteenth century by the Sinclairs, the local lairds, and was used for conducting their business.

Main Street

MAP PAGE 60
Main St, Scalloway, ZE1 0TR. Free.
Walking down Main Street toward the west end of town, there are a couple of historic points of interest to keep an eye out for. Dinapore House, a vaguely castle-like building just next to the Midshore road sign, was the Shetland Bus operation's headquarters, and just across the road, in the centre of a parking area overlooking the harbour, is a Shetland Bus memorial. Opposite it stands the Muckle Kirk (Big Church), a handsome stone structure dating from the 1840s.

A short distance further on, you'll find the Prince Olav Slipway, built in 1942 and named after Norway's Crown Prince, who visited during the site's construction. This was the main launch point for the Shetland Bus operations, which needed the capability to handle large fishing boats for its clandestine missions. Prior to the construction of the slipway, this area had been the centre of Scalloway's herring industry. A few steps further and you'll reach the red-brown Norway House, built in the nineteenth century and requisitioned in World War II to house the Norwegians running Shetland Bus missions.

Port Arthur
MAP PAGE 60
Port Arthur, ZE1 0UN. Free.

The road from Scalloway ends at the little settlement of Port Arthur, at the western end of the bay. From a gate off a residential street, there's a short out-and-back walk to the Pund lighthouse, following an easy track along the coastline, with lovely views across to Trondra and Burra. It should take about 45 minutes to walk to the lighthouse and back, and is a light and easy route which offers some splendid coastal scenery.

Trondra
MAP PAGE 58
Trondra, ZE1 0XL. Free.

From the Mainland, just outside Scalloway, you can cross a bridge to the island of Trondra, an attractive grassy place which has no specific sights, but offers lovely views as you head through. In particular, as you cross the bridge from Mainland, look north to get a fine panorama of Scalloway Castle. From Trondra, a further bridge connects to the island of West Burra.

Fugla Ness
MAP PAGE 58
Hamnavoe, West Burra, ZE2 9LA. Free.

A short and enjoyable walk begins at the village of Hamnavoe in West Burra's northwest corner. From the main road, head south on Duke Street until you see a yellow-brown house on your right. A track runs in front of this house onto the headland, becoming an obvious path that leads towards the Fugla Ness lighthouse, with attractive views of the harbour. The path is easy except for two points when you cross boulder fields, over which you'll need to be surefooted. It should take you around twenty minutes to reach the lighthouse, at which point you'll enjoy panoramic views of the islands all around the coast, and on clear days as far as Foula to the west.

Meal Beach
MAP PAGE 58
Hamnavoe, West Burra, ZE2 9LB. Free.

A solid contender for Shetland's best beach, Meal is flanked by small cliffs of jagged black rock, and boasts white sand and a clear sea which – but for the temperature – could put you in mind of the Caribbean. A good gravel path leads down from a dedicated car park, and should you wish to extend the walk you can pick up a path from the beach's western end, which leads around to Fugla Ness.

St Laurence Kirk
MAP PAGE 58
Papil, West Burra, ZE2 9UY. Free.

The church in Papil village, now missing its roof, dates back to the twelfth century, and is likely to have been a site of significance even before that. It was here that in 1887 the ninth-century Pictish

Meal Beach

Bannaminn Beach

Papil Stone was discovered, along with two other early Christian carved stones. The Papil Stone is now in Edinburgh's National Museum of Scotland, but there's a replica here in the churchyard.

Shetland Pony Experience

MAP PAGE 58
Papil, West Burra, ZE2 9UY. http://the shetlandponyexperience.com. Charge.
For an in-depth session learning about Shetland's iconic ponies, you won't find a better place than the Shetland Pony Experience. A visit lasts about 90 minutes, including an informative and engaging talk about the ponies, followed by the opportunity to stroke and brush them, and then take them on a short walk along the coast to a pretty beach. Children can enjoy a short ride on the ponies. Advance booking required.

Easthouse Museum

MAP PAGE 58
Papil, West Burra, ZE2 9LD. Free.
Closed for renovation at time of writing but expected to reopen for the 2025 summer season, the Easthouse Museum can be found in a thatched crofthouse on the outskirts of Papil. Its exhibition is likely to showcase items of local historical interest.

Bannaminn Beach

MAP PAGE 58
Papil, West Burra, ZE2 9LD. Free.
At the southern end of West Burra is Bannaminn Beach, a gorgeous stretch of fine white sand and calm, clear water. Running along behind it is a causeway which connects to the semi-island of Kettla Ness, around which you can walk in about two hours. It's an unchallenging but very pretty route, on which you'll have a good chance of seeing seals and seabirds – including Arctic skuas and terns, so be wary in nesting season.

The Outpost

MAP PAGE 58
Meadows Rd, Houss, East Burra, ZE2 9LE. http://facebook.com/TheOutpostShetlandIslands. Free, donations welcome.
Across on East Burra, you'll find the Outpost, a small menagerie run by an Tasmanian ex-pat, at which you can enjoy the incongruous sight of wallabies hopping around a field in Shetland. You'll also see emus, tortoises, pigs and a variety of birds, and will sometimes have the opportunity to feed the animals.

Houss Ness

MAP PAGE 58
Houss, East Burra, ZE2 9LE. Free.
The southern end of East Burra mirrors that of West Burra, with a beach acting as a causeway across to a semi-island, in this case Houss Ness. The beach here is smaller and stony rather than sandy, but the walk around Houss Ness is lovely, offering views of the brooding mass of Mainland to the east and West Burra to the west.

Papa Stour

Accessed by ferry from West Burrafirth, on the north coast of Westside, Papa Stour is Shetland's ninth largest island. It doesn't tend to draw many tourists, but that's not for want of interesting attractions: the island offers both historical sites and natural scenery for those who make the effort to reach it.

Even before you've disembarked the ferry, you'll spot some of Papa Stour's marvellous scenery: on the approach to the harbour of Housa Voe are a collection of splendid sea stacks, the tallest of which – Muckle Fru – is the subject of a legend concerning a Norwegian princess marooned here by her father, Lord Thorvald Thoresson, after she fell in love with a local fisherman. Naturally, the fisherman proved adept at scaling the stack and rescuing the princess, an outcome which Thorvald ought to have seen coming.

Further round the island, even more dramatic sea stacks can be seen on the west coast of Papa Stour, with the view over Aisha Stack being one of Shetland's most picturesque. The coastline here is especially rugged, with the sea having created gorgeous inlets and caves, ideal for exploring by kayak – get in touch with a company such as Sea Kayak Shetland (www.seakayakshetland.co.uk) to arrange a trip. It's also a fine spot to look out for seals and seabirds: Papa Stour is particularly known for its Arctic terns in the nesting season.

Papa Stour also has much to offer the archeologist: it's been inhabited for at least 5000 years, and there are remains from all eras of settlement from the Neolithic era to the modern day. The most interesting is perhaps the Norse-era house at Da Biggins, which is thought to be where Shetland's oldest surviving document – dating back to 1299 – was written. This document concerned Thorvald Thoressen, who, not content with imprisoning his daughter on a sea stack, also managed to get himself accused of corruption.

Relatively small though it is, Papa Stour is well worth a trip. There are usually two ferries per day at reasonable intervals, allowing you to explore the island for several hours before making the return trip. If you want to stay longer, accommodation is limited but the East Biggins crofthouse can sometimes be booked on Airbnb. There are no places to eat and no shops, so take all supplies with you.

---

of woodland ideal for visits with children. The paths through the trees reveal something new at every turn: toy boats, a flower fairy garden, even several dinosaurs. The woodland is dedicated to the memory of Michael Ferrie, a local musician who sadly passed away in 1996, aged just 21.

Vementry

MAP PAGE 66
Off B9071, ZE2 9ND.

The road from Aith towards Vementry is an absolute joy, offering a picturesque drive – or long walk – through undulating hills and past scenic lochs. At the end you'll be rewarded by views over a sea dotted with little islands to Vementry, no longer inhabited but home to remains dating back at least 4000 years. For the best views, head through the access gate next to the gate marked 'private', and follow the fence

Westside

ATLANTIC OCEAN

Papa Stour Ferry Terminal
HURDIBACK
BIGGINGS
Papa Stour
Sound of Papa
Ness of Melby — MELBY
SANDNESS — NORBY — GARTH
Huxter
Voe of Sharraness
Isle of West Burrafirth
WEST BURRAFIRTH
Houlma Wa
Snara Ness
West Burrafirth Ferry Terminal
Sandness Hill (616ft)
Mousavord Loch
Loch of Kellister
Loch of Hollorin
Bay of Deepdale — Deepdale
Burga Water
Sulma Water
DALE
Nu Ness
Voe of Dale
DALE OF WALLS
Stourborough (567ft)
Lunga Water
Loch of Flatpunds
Loch of Voxterby
Scord of Brouster
BRIDGE OF WALES
THE HAA
BRUNATWATT
BROWLAND
Wats Ness
Loch of Bardister
Loch Kirkgarth
WALLS
STOVE
Voe of Browland
GRUTIN
Woe of Footabrough
Walls Ferry Terminal
Loch of Grunnavoe
Braga Ness
Ness Grutin
Linga
Gruting Voe
N
Wester Sound
Easter Sound
Vaila
Ram's Head
Foula
CULSWICK
Culswick Broch

| 0 | kilometres | 3 |
| 0 | miles | 2 |

● **CAFÉ**
The Original Cake Fridge 1

● **SHOP**
Silly Sheep Fibre Company 1

■ **ACCOMMODATION**
Burrastow House 1
Skeld Caravan Park and Campsite 2

67

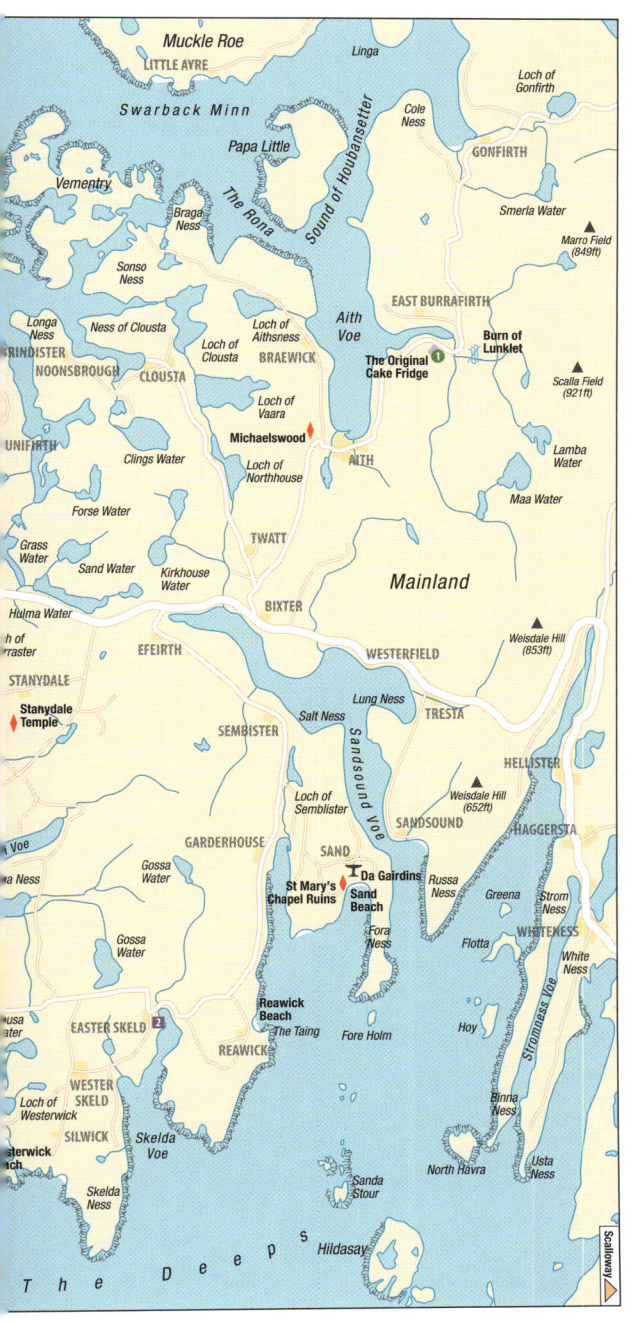

WESTSIDE

Muckle Roe
Little Ayre
Linga
Loch of Gonfirth
Swarback Minn
Papa Little
Cole Ness
Gonfirth
Vementry
The Rona
Sound of Houbansetter
Smerla Water
Braga Ness
Marro Field (849ft)
Sonso Ness
Loch of Aithsness
Aith Voe
East Burrafirth
Burn of Lunklet
Longa Ness
Ness of Clousta
Braewick
The Original Cake Fridge
Scalla Field (921ft)
Brindister
Noonsbrough
Loch of Clousta
Clousta
Loch of Vaara
Michaelswood
Unifirth
Clings Water
Aith
Loch of Northhouse
Lamba Water
Forse Water
Twatt
Maa Water
Grass Water
Sand Water
Kirkhouse Water
Hulma Water
Bixter
Mainland
h of rraster
Efeirth
Westerfield
Weisdale Hill (853ft)
Stanydale
Stanydale Temple
Salt Ness
Lung Ness
Tresta
Sembister
Hellister
Loch of Sembister
Weisdale Hill (652ft)
Garderhouse
Sandsound
Haggersta
Voe
Gossa Water
Sand
Da Gairdins
St Mary's Chapel Ruins
Sand Beach
Russa Ness
Greena
Strom Ness
Whiteness
a Ness
Gossa Water
Fora Ness
Flotta
White Ness
usa ater
Reawick Beach
Easter Skeld
The Taing
Reawick
Fore Holm
Hoy
Stromness Voe
Wester Skeld
Silwick
Loch of Westerwick
Skelda Voe
Binna Ness
Usta Ness
terwick h
Skelda Ness
North Ravra
Sanda Stour
Hildasay
Scalloway
T h e   D e e p s

line, the panorama unfolding as you go.

The Original Cake Fridge

MAP PAGE 66
B9071, East Burrafirth,
ZE2 9NE. http://facebook.com/
theoriginalcakefridgeandtearoom.
Across Shetland you'll often come across honesty boxes selling hot drinks and cakes, a trend started by this place just north of Aith. Established in 2012, it quickly became famous – including via an appearance on the *Shetland* TV show – and now attracts plenty of visitors. The fridge itself, packed with goodies, is open 24/7, and there's also a tearoom and craft shop if you're passing by during regular business hours.

Burn of Lunklet

MAP PAGE 66
Off B9071, East Burrafirth, ZE2 9NE.
A delightful short stroll begins from a parking area about five hundred metres from the Original Cake Fridge. Simply follow the easy gravel path alongside the burn, past little cascades as it bubbles down from the hills ahead. Keep to the left when you reach a bridge, and after rounding a corner you'll see a beautiful waterfall. The whole walk, out and back, should take you about 20 minutes.

West Burrafirth

MAP PAGE 66
Off A971, West Burrafirth, ZE2 9NT.
There's not a whole lot more to West Burrafirth than the small pier from which you can pick up the ferry to Papa Stour, but even if you're not headed to the island, it's worth a diversion up this very pretty road, which threads through an undulating landscape dotted with lochs. This is gorgeous

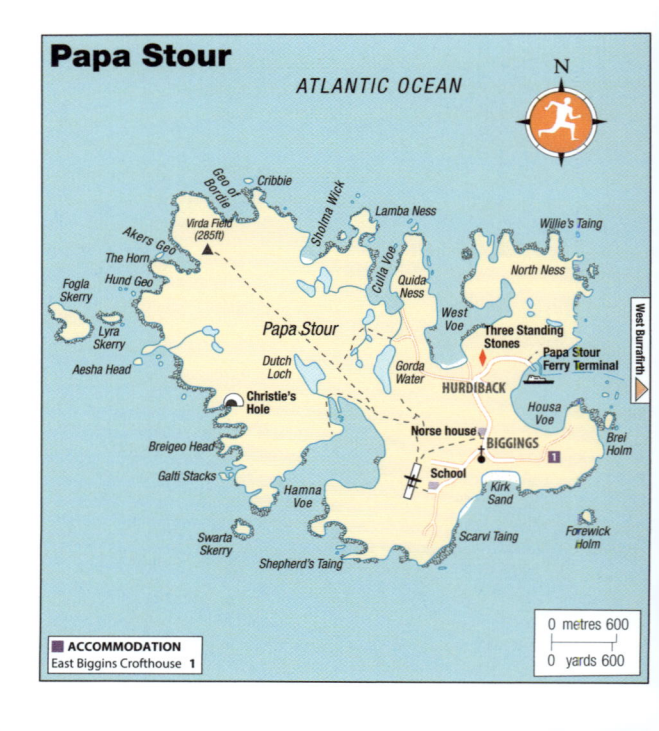

Foula

Foula, Shetland's eighth largest island, is one of the UK's most isolated inhabited islands. Visible on the horizon from much of the west coast of Westside, it takes 2hr 15min to reach by passenger ferry from Walls, with sailings every two to three days. Note that it's not possible to make a day trip by ferry: if you only have a day, you'll need to take a flight from Tingwall Airport. Flight bookings must be made by phone (01595 840246) or email (lwk.ops@airtask.com). If you wish to stay overnight, there are a couple of accommodation options, but it's essential to book ahead. Also note that there is no shop or café on the island.

Foula's isolation has shaped much of its history: it has been settled since Neolithic times, and may have been the island the Romans regarded as 'ultima Thule', the furthest known northern point in the world. It is thought to have existed largely independently of Norwegian rule, and was one of the last hold-outs of the now extinct Norn language which was once spoken across Shetland. Even today, its isolation is emphasised by it being the only place in the UK which has not adopted the Gregorian calendar, instead having continued to use the Julian system since 1752.

Making the journey to Foula may take you to the edge of the world, but it's more than worth it. The island is ideal for birdwatching – the name 'Foula' is derived from the Old Norse for 'bird island' – with some of the UK's tallest cliffs providing excellent nesting for a huge variety and number of seabirds, including Arctic terns, great skuas, puffins, fulmars and more.

The rugged cliffs also make splendid terrain for walking – the climb up to the summit of Foula's tallest hill, the Kame, is an excellent hike. Other routes include a shorter walk at the north end of the island to view the Gaada Stack, a beautiful natural arch just offshore; and the out-and-back hike to the magnificently named Sneck Ida Smaalie gully.

If you prefer to get in the sea rather than looking at it, Foula offers some spectacular diving. Check out http://shetland.org/visit/do/outdoors/dive to find a company, with trips possible to the wreck site of the RMS *Oceanic*, a sister ship of the *Titanic*, which unfortunately sank off Foula after being pressed into naval service in the early days of World War I.

walking country – take the coastal path and explore.

Scord of Brouster
MAP PAGE 66
A971, Bridge of Walls, ZE2 9NP.
The ancient site of the Scord of Brouster isn't as dramatic in appearance as other Stone Age ruins on Shetland – with little to look at except some scattered stones in the approximate shape of buildings – but it's an important one, as it's thought to be among the earliest settlements yet discovered here, dating from around 3000 BC. Start by climbing to the information board above the site, where you can make out the house outlines more easily, then descend to take a closer look.

Sandness
MAP PAGE 66
A971, Sandness, ZE2 9PL.
The community of Sandness is fairly spread out, with

intermittent clusters of houses periodically found along the seafront. The village boasts not just one but two fine sandy beaches with great views of Papa Stour opposite: they're both very pretty but arguably the pick of the pair is the eastern one, thanks to its wide sweep of strikingly orange sand and the dramatic cliff. Sandness is also home to Jamieson's Spinning Mill, which produces iconic Shetland wool, sold in their Lerwick shop (see page 32).

Huxter
MAP PAGE 66
Off A971, Huxter, ZE2 9PL.
A short and well-signposted coastal walk from the settlement of Huxter, just west of Sandness, leads to a trio of abandoned water mills, which were powered by the burn flowing down from the nearby Loch of Huxter. They are known to date from at least the mid-nineteenth century, but it's thought they may have been built as long ago as the Norse era. You can pick up the spectacular coast path here and approach Deepdale from the north as an alternative to the route outlined on page 70.

Deepdale
MAP PAGE 66
Off A971, Dale of Wells, ZE2 9PE.
One of the finest walks on Shetland can be enjoyed along the northwest coast of Westside. Head to Dale of Wells and, starting from the parking area as the road bends south to Wells, follow the track down to Voe of Dale beach. Once there, admire the distinctive stepped cliffs of Foula, visible directly ahead, before taking the path up along the coast to your right.

It's initially a bit of a steep ascent, but once you're at the top of the cliffs, you stay at more or less this elevation for the rest of the route. Simply follow the coastline, enjoying the stunning panoramas as they open up before you, with the sea crashing upon the jagged rocks and headlands of the cliffs.

After about three kilometres, you'll reach the top of a rise and see a particularly large cliff ahead, with its bare grey face sloping

Culswick Broch

steeply down to the sea. The bay it surrounds is Deepdale, a beautiful stony beach with turquoise waters, which can only be admired from above. To get closer, you'll need to descend into the ravine of a burn, then climb the other side.

A second, much deeper, gully awaits, but the views are superb from here, so you don't need to head down unless you're planning on making this a much longer walk: if you have boundless energy and plenty of time, you could continue all the way round to Sandness, or alternatively cut inland and ascend Sandness Hill before heading south to loop back to the walk's start point. It's easiest, though, to simply treat this as an out-and-back walk, and retrace your steps from Deepdale along the coast.

Walls

MAP PAGE 66
A971, Walls, ZE2 9PH.
The attractive village of Walls is one of the main settlements at this end of Westside. It stretches around a small, sheltered bay, and is the terminal for the ferry to Foula. Otherwise, it's best known for sailing – check out the Regatta Club (http://facebook.com/WallsRegattaClub) to find out about upcoming events.

Stanydale Temple

MAP PAGE 66
Off A971, ZE2 9NR.
http://historicenvironment.scot/visit-a-place/places/stanydale-temple.
A trail of about a kilometre, marked by black and white poles over often boggy ground, starts from a roadside parking spot and leads to Stanydale Temple, the remains of a Neolithic building dating back perhaps 5000 years. It's referred to as a temple, owing to its similarity to contemporary temples found in Malta, and it's certainly possible that it was used for religious ceremonies, though its precise purpose is unknown.

Whatever its usage, though, it's one of the largest and best-

Burn of Lunklet

preserved Neolithic buildings in Shetland, and must have been extremely impressive in its day. Inside, you can see large alcoves which may have been separate chambers, and several hearth areas in the centre. It's likely to have been at the heart of a settlement, as there are remains of smaller buildings nearby. One such is just next to one of the black and white poles on the path to the temple; due to the lie of the land, it's easy to miss on the way, but you'll spot it without difficulty on the walk back.

Culswick Broch

MAP PAGE 66
Off B9071, ZE2 9NL.
Culswick Broch might just be the most dramatically sited of all Shetland's brochs: set on a high hill between a loch and the sea, it's an imposing sight, and would have been even more so in its heyday. It's still more complete than many brochs: its walls are low but intact, and there's even a surviving alcove into which you can peer to appreciate the

thickness of the walls. Earthworks run around its base, adding to its impregnable defences. The 360-degree view from the summit is nothing short of spectacular, with the rugged coast of Westside on show and Foula looming on the western horizon.

It's a walk of about two kilometres to get to the broch: once in Culswick, start from the track signed to Culswick Methodist Chapel and follow it through another gate marked 'Footpath to Sotersta and Pictish Broch'. It's an easy track to follow, threading round the north and west of Sotersta Loch and then round the Loch of the Brough. At the top of a rise, the track disappears, but you can see the broch on your left now: just head towards it, descending to cross a causeway and then yomping steeply uphill to the broch. Despite the tempting track that descends the opposite side of the broch, the gates in the field here are often locked, preventing you from making a loop round the Loch of the Brough – it's easier to return by the route you came.

Westerwick Beach

MAP PAGE 66
Off B9071, Westerwick, ZE2 9NL.

The stony beach at Westerwick is a lovely spot to admire some of this region's dramatic coastal scenery. From the beach, you can see stacks and pillars in the sea, and there are enjoyable walks starting here which head around the cliffs offering further great views.

Reawick Beach

MAP PAGE 66
Off B9071, Reawick, ZE2 9NJ.

The small Reawick Beach sits in an attractive little cove, and offers relatively coarse orange sand, with calm and beautifully clear water. It's well worth a stop on a sunny day.

Westerwick

Sand Beach
MAP PAGE 66
Off B9071, Sand, ZE2 9NQ.
No prizes for guessing whether this beach is stony or sandy: it is of course a sandy beach, and a very pretty one at that, with gently lapping waves and views out over little islands. Just next to the beach are the picturesque ruins of the twelfth-century St Mary's Chapel, while on the hill behind the churchyard is Sand Haa, one of Shetland's few eighteenth-century laird's homes to still be inhabited.

Da Gairdins
MAP PAGE 66
Off B9071, Sand, ZE2 9NQ.
http://gairdins.org.uk.
If you're hankering after trees, consider a stop at Da Gairdins, a beautifully maintained area of woodland and gardens, overlooking Sand Beach. It's a splendid place for a wander through the trees, across the lawns, and round the ponds down to the small loch. It can be quite a surprise to happen upon the grove of palm trees thriving in Shetland.

Shop

Silly Sheep Fibre Company
MAP PAGE 66
A971, Walls, ZE2 9PF.
http://sillysheepfibrecompany.com.
There's a flock of about fifty sheep at the Silly Sheep croft, and their wool provides the raw material for the lovely many coloured wools available at this shop. It's best to get in touch in advance if you want to call by.

Café

The Original Cake Fridge
MAP PAGE 66
B9071, East Burrafirth, ZE2 9NE. http://facebook.com/theoriginalcakefridgeandtearoom.
This iconic Shetland destination is worth the trip: it's a great little tearoom, serving tea, coffee and some of the most incredibly tempting cakes you're ever likely to see. Light lunches are also sometimes available, but check in advance. £

Northeast Mainland

Northeastern Mainland is composed of three districts, which south to north are known as Nesting, Lunnasting and Delting. Lunnasting in particular is home to some marvellous coastal scenery, and also boasts a fascinating wartime history. Nesting too offers gorgeous walking territory, especially around Gletness. Delting, meanwhile, is home to the large village of Brae, the gateway to the Northmavine area as well as the island of Muckle Roe, on which you can enjoy one of Shetland's finest and most popular walking routes.

Girlsta Loch

MAP PAGE 76
A970, Girlsta, ZE2 9SQ. Free.

Girlsta Loch, on your right as you drive north along the A970, is large enough that you could easily mistake it for the sea at first glance. This moody body of water, best admired from a small parking area at its southern end, is Shetland's deepest loch, and home to a unique subspecies of the Arctic char fish. It takes its name from Geirhildr, a Viking princess who drowned in the loch in the ninth century.

Kergord

Kergord

MAP PAGE 76
B9075, Setter, ZE2 9LW. Free.

A quick diversion from the A970 just north of Girlsta will bring you to Kergord, Shetland's largest patch of woodland. Though it's not an enormous forest, it contains a few short paths to roam through the woods, and can be a tonic to anyone who's missing the sight of trees. Kergord House, by the roadside here, was used as a headquarters during the Shetland Bus operation (see page 59).

Bonhoga Gallery

MAP PAGE 76
B9075, Weisdale Mill, Weisdale, ZE2 9LW.
http://shetlandarts.org/venues/bonhoga.
Free.

Closed for renovation at time of writing, but expected to reopen in 2025, the Bonhoga Gallery occupies the attractive nineteenth-century stone building of Weisdale Mill. It displays pieces by local artists, and also has a shop and café.

Girlsta to Laxo

MAP PAGE 76
B9075, ZE2 9PS. Free.

Just north of Girlsta Loch, the B9075 heads east to Skellister, a little village with houses built in a handsome Nordic style sat at the head of a picturesque bay. If you're travelling by car, it's well worth the short drive from here along

The Lunnasting Stone

In 1876, in a peat bog north of the Cabin Museum, a large stone was discovered, bearing mysterious carved inscriptions. On closer examination, it was found that the carvings were in ogham, an early medieval writing system used for transcribing Old Irish. Experts disagree on the dating of the Lunnasting Stone, with theories ranging from the sixth to the ninth centuries, and translation has also proved challenging. It is now on display in the National Museum of Scotland in Edinburgh.

the Gletness peninsula: the road threads through bleakly pretty hills and moorland, terminating at a small parking area. Here, a sign labelled 'Access to shore' points you to the beach, which is stony and looks out over a sea dotted with gorgeous small islands.

The entire coastal road from Gletness to Laxo is a delight to drive, with worthwhile stops at the Mull of Eswick – from which you'll get beautiful views across the sea – and at Neap, where you can take walks along the coast with an excellent chance of seeing seabirds, including puffins.

The Cabin Museum
MAP PAGE 76
B9071, Laxo, ZE2 9QD. 01595 694891. Free.
The main reason for a visit to Laxo is to pick up the ferry to Whalsay, which departs at regular intervals, but it's also home to the Cabin Museum. This little place near the Laxo ferry terminal houses one man's enormous collection of military memorabilia, which he began in 1970 and continued to build on until his death in 2007. It's an astonishing array, of particular interest for the many regimental badges and uniforms. Though the bulk of the displays are military focused, items of other provenance include artefacts from the whaling industry, early twentieth-century wedding dresses and even a 1920s guidebook to Shetland. It's all immaculately displayed and laid out with informative labels, and you'll find it surprisingly easy to get absorbed in the collection for longer than you might expect.

Vidlin
MAP PAGE 76
B9071, Laxo, ZE2 9QB. Free.
The little village of Vidlin has a harbour from which ferries to the Out Skerries sail, and is occasionally used as an alternative departure point for the Whalsay ferry. If you find yourself here, take a quick look at the church next to the ferry terminal: the adjacent grassy mound is an unexcavated Iron Age broch.

Lunna
MAP PAGE 76
B9071, Laxo, ZE2 9QF. Free.
Following the road north from Vidlin will bring you to Lunna, a small settlement found at the narrowest point of the Lunna Ness peninsula. It was here, in 1941, that the Shetland Bus operations began, before moving to their more famous base at Scalloway the following year. Lunna House, a grand seventeenth-century building atop a small hill, was used as the operation's headquarters.

Lunna's history goes back much further than World War II, though: in fact, the village's Lunna Kirk is thought to be the site of the oldest place of Christian worship on Shetland. Although the current incarnation of the church dates only to 1753, it seems that the site may have been in use by Christians even before the Viking era. Today's church is an attractive white building, perched on a headland

Northeast Mainland

77

NORTHEAST MAINLAND

PUBS	
Mid Brae Inn	2
Northern Lights	3
Welcome Inn	1

SHOP	
Hatchery Bookshop	1

ACCOMMODATION	
Brae Hotel	2
Busta House Hotel	3
Voxter Outdoor Centre	1

RESTAURANTS AND CAFÉS	
Busta House Hotel	2
Frankie's Fish and Chips	1

and overlooked by the dour facade of Lunna House.

Lunna Ness
MAP PAGE 76
B9071, Laxo, ZE2 9QF. Free.

The Lunna Ness headland offers some of Shetland's best walking: it's a gorgeous rugged peninsula with undulating rises and dips, dotted with rocky crags and little lochs, and boasting splendid views out over the sea. A particular highlight is the ramble to the Stones of Stofast, which you can pick up from a marked stile on the Lunna Ness road past the settlement of Hamnavoe. Strike out across the often boggy moor to eventually reach the dramatic large boulders, split into pieces by the effects of many years of alternate freezing and thawing – though, of course, local legend offers more supernatural explanations for the formation of these eye-catching landmarks.

Voe
MAP PAGE 76
A970, Voe, ZE2 9PX. Free.

Anyone travelling in Shetland's north is likely to pass through the village of Voe at some point: it connects routes to the south, Westside, Northmavine and the ferry terminal for Yell, Unst and Fetlar. The village itself is an attractive little place, stretched around the bay at the head of Olnafirth. It's most famous as the home of Adie's of Voe, the producers of the jumpers that Edmund Hillary and Tenzing Norgay wore for their successful ascent of Everest in 1953.

Toft
MAP PAGE 76
A968, Toft, ZE2 9QT. Free.

From Voe, the A968 runs north to Toft, notable largely for its ferry terminal which offers access to the northern islands of Yell, Unst and Fetlar. There are few facilities at Toft itself, but the nearby village of Mossbank is worth a stop for a visit to the friendly Welcome Inn pub.

Burn of Valayre
MAP PAGE 76
B9076, ZE2 9SW. Free.

Not signposted from the road (look for a parking area by a bridge about a kilometre south of Voxter Outdoor Centre), this offers a rare woodland walk. The short path alongside the trickling burn has been planted with trees as a community project, making for a lovely five-minute stroll ascending to a viewpoint over a pretty waterfall. If you're in the mood for a longer walk, the path continues past the edge of the woodland and up into the hills.

Brae
MAP PAGE 76
A970, ZE2 9QG. Free.

Brae, one of Shetland's larger villages, grew rapidly following the construction of the Sullom Voe oil terminal, and now boasts some of the best facilities you'll find outside Lerwick, including a large hotel, two pubs, a fish and chip shop, a petrol garage and a convenience store. It is the gateway to Northmavine, and is a good place to stock up on supplies if you're planning lengthy walks on the rugged northern peninsula.

Muckle Roe
MAP PAGE 76
A970, ZE2 9QW. Free.

The small island of Muckle Roe is connected to Mainland via a bridge just outside Brae, and is home to some spectacular coastal scenery. The classic Muckle Roe route is to the island's lighthouse, starting from a car park at the end of the island's road. Walkers can follow the coast from here along excellent and well-marked tracks, involving some relatively steep ascents and descents, past splendid views over the undulating hills of Westside. You can extend the walk further round the coastline, reaching a pretty point known as the Hams, before cutting back inland to the walk's start point.

Shop

Hatchery Bookshop

MAP PAGE 76
B9075, Weisdale, ZE2 9LW.
http://hatcherybookshop.kergord.co.uk.
A cosy little shop just opposite the Bonhoga Gallery, the Hatchery has a great selection of second-hand books to browse. The enthusiastic owner regularly changes a display of featured books depending on current Shetland events: Wool Week, for example, will be showcased with a selection of books on knitwear.

Restaurant

Busta House Hotel

MAP PAGE 76
Busta, ZE2 9QN.
http://bustahouse.com/restaurant.
This restaurant has a great menu of delicious, locally sourced dishes. The lamb in honey and mint sauce is particularly excellent. There's also what has to be Shetland's best wine list, with vintages from all the usual suspects (Italy, France, Argentina and so on) plus more unexpected sources: Lebanon, Moldova and Georgia, among others. The staff really know their wines and can help you pair perfectly with your meal. Book in advance. ££££

Café

Frankie's Fish and Chips

MAP PAGE 76
A970, Brae, ZE2 9QJ.
http://frankiesfishandchips.com.
Britain's most northerly fish and chip shop is found in Brae, and has both a sit-in café and a takeaway option. The fish and chips are just perfect – crispy, golden batter enclosing soft, flavoursome fish, accompanied by delicious chips. The only complaint is the short opening hours: they close at 7pm. ££

Busta House Hotel

Pubs

Mid Brae Inn

MAP PAGE 76
A970, Brae, ZE2 9QJ.
http://tinyurl.com/midbraeinn.
An often lively local pub, bordering on grungy, and an enjoyable spot for a beer or whisky. Evening meals of pub grub are usually available too. Enter via the side entrance.

Northern Lights

MAP PAGE 76
A970, Brae, ZE2 9QJ. http://braehotel.co.uk/the-northern-lights-bar.
A friendly bar adjoining the Brae Hotel, this is a popular local hangout, with a well-stocked bar and a good indie-rock soundtrack.

Welcome Inn

MAP PAGE 76
Mossbank, ZE2 9RB. http://facebook.com/WelcomeInnMossbank.
A very friendly pub in Mossbank, with a good range of beers, a pool table, and regular fun events such as bingo. In 2023, it was named Shetland's best pub.

Whalsay and Out Skerries

Whalsay might be a small island, but it's got a larger population than bigger contenders such as Unst and Yell. This is down to its fishing industry, which has made the island prosperous over the centuries. It makes a worthy day trip: with two museums, some fascinating Neolithic remains to seek out on a pretty coastal walk, and the UK's northernmost golf course, there's a variety of activities to keep you busy. The tiny islands of Out Skerries, meanwhile, lie some distance eastward of Whalsay, and boast some fine walking country and wildlife-spotting opportunities.

Symbister
MAP PAGE 80
Symbister, ZE2 9AA. Free.
Whalsay ferries arrive into Symbister, a busy little harbour village which is also home to the island's two museums. It has a long history, which revolves around its fishing industry, principally herring and whitefish.

Pier House Museum
MAP PAGE 80
Symbister, ZE2 9AA. Charge.
At the east end of Symbister's harbour stands a little stone

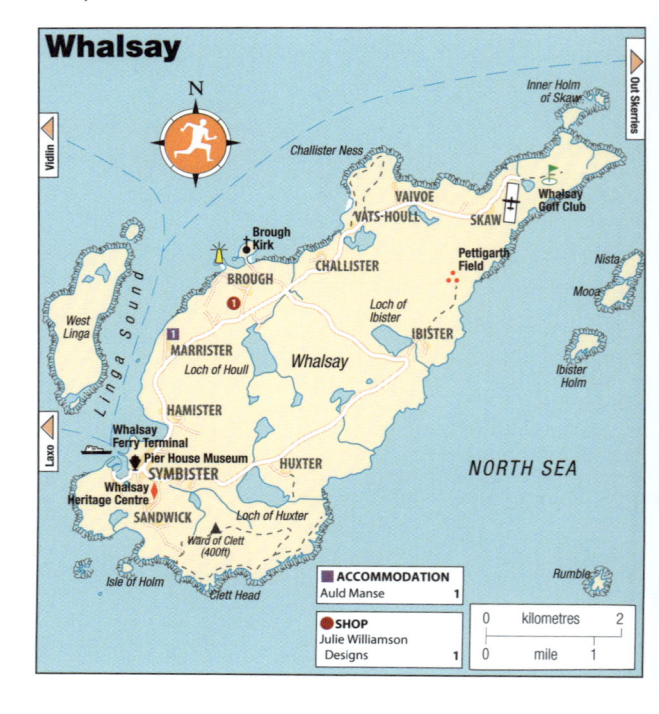

Symbister harbour

building known as the Pier House. Dating back perhaps as far as the sixteenth century, it was used and possibly built by merchants from the Hanseatic League, who dominated trade in northern Europe during the medieval period. Inside, there's a little exhibition on the history of the building itself, as well as the wider picture of Hanseatic League activities around Whalsay and across Europe. The keys for the museum can be picked up from the shop across the road. Mind your head when entering: the door to the ground floor is particularly low.

Whalsay Heritage Centre
MAP PAGE 80

Symbister, ZE2 9AB. http://whalsayheritage.co.uk. Charge.
The excellent Whalsay Heritage Centre is well worth a visit to get a grounding in the subject that has been most important to this island over the centuries: fishing. The museum's main exhibition is to your right on entry, offering a detailed look at the history of the fishing industry in Whalsay, from the Hanseatic era all the way to the modern day. As well as a wealth of information, photographs and model ships, there's also a marvellous collection of artefacts, from hooks and ropes to ornate boat clocks and a splendid 1950s radio. The museum's other room hosts annually changing temporary

Getting to Whalsay

Ferries to Whalsay leave from one of two harbours on the northeastern Mainland – it's usually Laxo, but sometimes Vidlin is used instead. There are LED road signs on the A970 to tell you which harbour to make for. Departures are roughly every 45 minutes, and the sailing takes about 30 minutes. Ferries take both foot passengers and cars.

Ferry arriving at the Skerries

exhibitions, with past subjects including the weaving of Shetland cloth. The centre also has a small gift shop, and can rustle up a cup of coffee or tea.

The Heritage Centre is housed in the outbuildings of Symbister House, an extremely grand structure considered Shetland's most impressive Georgian mansion. Built in the 1820s by the local landlords, the Bruces, it remained their family home until the 1940s. From the 1960s onwards, it was used as the island's school.

Ward of Clett
MAP PAGE 80
Clate, ZE2 9AG. Free.
Ascending to Whalsay's highest point is a relatively short and easy walk, which you can begin either by walking the road from Symbister to the settlement of Clate or, if you fancy a quicker outing, from Clate itself. The track from Clate is easy to pick up, and it heads up the hill on a switchback route. The summit is marked by a trig point.

Loch of Huxter
MAP PAGE 80
Huxter, ZE2 9AH. Free.
In Whalsay's southeast is the Loch of Huxter, a pretty body of water which sits beneath the Ward of Clett. Just off its southern shore, the ruins of an Iron Age island fort can still be seen. Though less complete, it is similar to the fort ruins at Clickimin (see page 29) and the Ness of Burgi (see page 48).

Pettigarth Field
MAP PAGE 80
Access from Isbister, ZE2 9AJ. Free.
Pettigarth Field contains Whalsay's most significant Neolithic remains: several houses and a chambered tomb, all of which were excavated in the mid-twentieth century. Reachable on foot, the ruins are plain to see, if you know where to find them: unfortunately there are few signposts pointing the way. Start the walk at the village of

Ferries to the Skerries

The Out Skerries can be reached by ferry from several harbours across Shetland, though sailings aren't frequent: for the most part, there will be only one departure from each of the harbours per day. The shortest route is from Symbister on Whalsay, which takes 75 minutes, but obviously requires getting to Whalsay first; options from the Mainland include from Vidlin (90 minutes) and Lerwick (150 minutes). The ferries carry both foot passengers and cars, but the Out Skerries are small enough that you may feel taking the car is unnecessary.

Isbister: once past Isbister Loch, take the left road at the T-junction and continue until the road ends, where you can park. The path begins to the left of the grey pebbledash house on the corner.

Pass through the gate – which has a map marked Pettigarth Field on it – and head up the gravel track. When the track ends at a gate, head right to skirt around an enclosed area, then pass through two gates and follow the path as it heads to a rise, bringing views of islets in the sea into view. After another gate on your left you'll climb further, making for a prominent boulder ahead. From this you can see a wooden post ahead: making for this, from the top of the next rise you can see a grey stone structure below. Head towards it, over sometimes boggy ground, and just adjacent you'll find the first of the Neolithic houses, known as Benie Hoose, a large multi-chambered structure which, when excavated, yielded a vast number of tools, including axes, pots and querns.

Walk directly east towards the sea and you'll find a smaller, less well preserved house, called Yoxie Geo. At time of excavation, it was thought that this may have been a temple, though later archeological thinking suggests that like Benie Hoose, it was a residence. Immediately above the Benie Hoose at the top of the hill are the foundations of a small burial cairn: you can still make out the entrance passageway and three tomb chambers.

You can either retrace your steps to Isbister, or continue along the coast from here to emerge at Whalsay's landing strip near the Skaw golf course, enjoying views of Out Skerries as you go. If you're a keen archeologist, check out the map at the Heritage Centre, which can point you in the direction of other ancient sites on Whalsay.

Brough Kirk
MAP PAGE 80
Brough, ZE2 9AL. Free.
Roughly halfway along the northern coast of Whalsay is

Brough Kirk Cemetery

Out Skerries

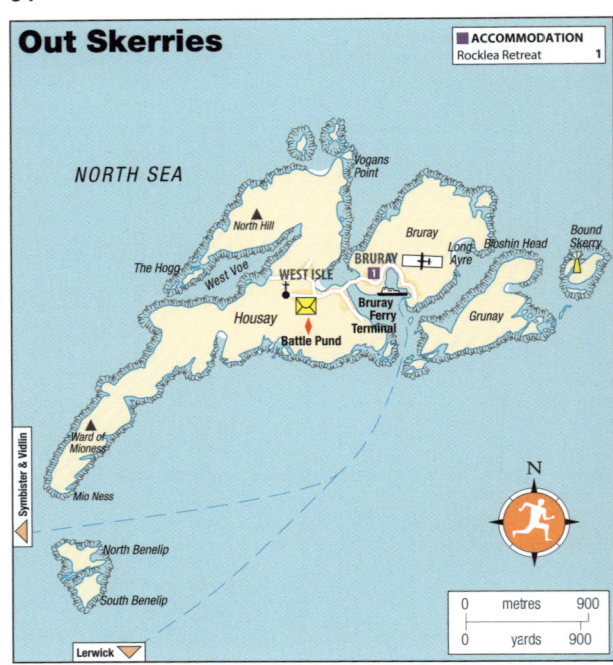

ACCOMMODATION
Rocklea Retreat — 1

the village of Brough, worth a quick stop to visit its kirk, which occupies a particularly impressive location on a small island, connected to Whalsay via a short causeway. It's a pretty spot, if an exposed one, giving good views up and down the rugged coast. The church itself is an old stone building, which at time of writing was undergoing restoration.

Whalsay Golf Club
MAP PAGE 80
Skaw, ZE2 9AW. http://whalsaygolfclub.co.uk. Charge.

The far northeast tip of the island is home to Whalsay Golf Club, a course nestled alongside the East Loch of Skaw. Although a decent place for a round, its main claim to fame is that it's Britain's most northerly golf club. If you don't fancy a game, you could instead take a walk around this headland to enjoy lovely views.

The Out Skerries

The small islands of the Out Skerries are dotted across the sea east of Whalsay, and are one of the least populated and least visited parts of Shetland. Making the effort to reach them is rewarding, with the Skerries offering fine walking and birdwatching opportunities, as well as the chance to tick off a visit to Scotland's most easterly point. They are composed of three main islands, Bruray, Housay and Grunay, of which Grunay is uninhabited.

Bruray
MAP PAGE 84
Bruray, ZE2 9AR. Free.

Ferries arrive at Bruray's harbour, which has been the centre of the Skerries' life for centuries: the economy here was long reliant on

Eating on Whalsay and the Out Skerries

There are no regularly open cafés, restaurants or pubs on Whalsay or the Out Skerries. Your best bet is the Auld Manse (Marrister, Whalsay, ZE2 9AE, http://facebook.com/AuldManseWhalsay), which opens on a pop-up basis – check the Facebook page to see if they will be open during your visit. Otherwise, the Heritage Centre in Whalsay can offer coffee, tea and biscuits for a small donation, and there are also coffee and tea-making facilities at the ferry terminal on Bruray. You can pick up picnic supplies from the small but well-stocked shops on the islands: JWJ (opposite the Pier House Museum) on Whalsay, and A Humphray General Stores on the Out Skerries.

the sea, including a stint under the haaf fishing system (see page 98). On the northeast side of the island is the beach of Long Ayre, which was once intensively used to dry fish catches before their export: you can still see the large stones on the beach where the fish were laid out for drying. Walking north from here will bring you to Bloshin Head, from which you can enjoy a view across to the lighthouse on Bound Skerry, Scotland's easternmost point.

Housay
MAP PAGE 84
Housay, ZE2 9AS. Free.

There are few ancient sites to seek out on the Out Skerries, but one exception is the Battle Pund, a Bronze Age stone circle, the purpose of which remains unknown. It can be found on the east side of Housay, not far from the bridge connecting the island with Bruray.

The principal reason to visit Housay – and indeed the Skerries – can be found in the island's southwestern corner, along the peninsula of Mio Ness. Taking in this finger of land on a circular walk is a delight, passing beautiful coastal scenery as you approach the site of an unexpected treasure hunt in the 1960s. It had long been known that the Dutch vessels *De Liefde* and the *Kennemerland* had been wrecked here in the seventeenth and eighteenth centuries, but in 1960 silver and gold coins from the ships were discovered on the shore. The ships were subsequently excavated, with the work on the *Kennemerland* being a pioneering exercise in maritime archeology.

Mio Ness has another historical maritime association – owing to its remote location, men would hide here to avoid the press gangs during the Napoleonic Wars era. On the southern side of the peninsula, you'll come across a stone known as Annie Elspeth's resting place: folklore has it that Annie would stop here to watch the horizon for ships, as she took food to men in hiding along Mio Ness.

Shop

Julie Williamson Designs
MAP PAGE 80
Brough, Whalsay, ZE2 9AL.
http://juliewilliamsondesigns.co.uk.

You'll find handmade Shetland-themed crafts and artwork at Julie's studio in Brough village: products range from lampshades and cushions to coasters and tea towels. For a unique Shetland souvenir, pop by, or order via the website.

Northmavine

Connected to the Mainland by a narrow strip of land known as Mavis Grind, the northwestern corner of Shetland is known as Northmavine. It's a wild and rugged place, where you'll find some of Shetland's most spectacular scenery, much of it accessed on relatively lengthy but not difficult walks. The coastal walk at the cliffs of Esha Ness is one of Shetland's highlights and should not be missed, but it's well worth also making time to explore Fethaland and Uyea Island, and – if it's a clear day – climbing to Shetland's highest summit, Ronas Hill.

Mavis Grind
MAP PAGE 88
A970, ZE2 9RE. Free.

You can't miss your arrival in the north, thanks to the large Hollywood-esque sign above the road welcoming you to Northmavine. The sign stands at Mavis Grind, a narrow isthmus connecting Shetland's Mainland to the northern peninsula, and separating the Atlantic Ocean and the North Sea by a mere fifty metres or so. The causeway shows signs of habitation for millennia, and it was used well into the twentieth century as a shortcut for boats, which were often carried over the land here to avoid making the long seaward journey around Northmavine.

Gunnister Man's Stone
MAP PAGE 88
Off A970, ZE2 9RE. Free.

Just off the A970 on the side road to Gunnister, a large stone marks the spot where, in 1951, two local peat cutters discovered the remains of a body now known as the Gunnister Man. Thought to date from around 1700, the Gunnister Man's clothing, purse and belongings survived in excellent condition thanks to the peat in which he was buried, offering interesting evidence of the development of Shetland knitwear. There's an informative display on the Gunnister Man in the Tangwick Haa Museum, though all of his personal effects found here are now on display in Edinburgh's National Museum of Scotland.

Shortly after the Gunnister turn-off, the road splits. Confusingly, both roads remain the A970, with the western branch heading to Hillswick, and the northern route pushing up to Fethaland.

Tangwick Haa Museum

Hillswick

MAP PAGE 88
Hillswick, ZE2 9RW. Free.

The village of Hillswick is a pleasant little place which in the past was big in the herring fishing industry. It has a pebble beach, a couple of shops, a seal sanctuary, and a large and rather dour church. It's also the start point for the Hillswick Circular, a seven-kilometre walk which circumnavigates the beautiful Ness of Hillswick peninsula. Allow two to three hours to walk the circuit.

Hillswick Seal Sanctuary

MAP PAGE 88
Hillswick, ZE2 9RW.
http://hillswickwildlifesanctuary.org. Free, donations welcome.

This donation-funded sanctuary rescues abandoned seal pups from across Shetland, housing them in seawater pools until they're ready for release back into the sea. You can visit to see the resident seals, and chat to the friendly staff, who are a mine of information about the different seal species native to Shetland. There's a small shop of seal-themed souvenirs, and donations are always welcomed.

Weaving Shed Gallery

MAP PAGE 88
Hillswick, ZE2 9RW.
http://weavingshedgallery.com/weavingshed. Free.

Open by appointment only, this small art gallery on Hillswick's beachfront hosts a permanent collection of paintings by Jeanette Obstoj, an artist who often holidayed in this part of Shetland and who is best known for writing lyrics for singers such as Tina Turner and Dusty Springfield. You may also find temporary exhibitions of pieces by local artists.

Tangwick Haa Museum

MAP PAGE 88
Off B9078, Esha Ness, ZE2 9RS.
http://tangwickhaa.org.uk. Free, donations welcome.

This local history museum on the Esha Ness peninsula has a wealth of exhibits, spread across three upstairs rooms. The room into which you ascend contains information on a variety of local interest topics, including the finding of the Gunnister Man (see page 86) and the career of Captain Andrew Cheyne, who grew up at nearby Stenness in the nineteenth century. The immediately adjacent Laird's Room is set up as a traditional nineteenth-century parlour, with plenty of furniture and ornaments to examine, while the room at the far end hosts annually changing temporary exhibitions, past subjects of which have included toys and wedding dresses.

Stenness

MAP PAGE 88
B9078, Stenness, ZE2 9RS. Free.

The headland of Stenness has some dramatic scenery to explore, shaped by the volcanic past of the region. You can admire it on a short coastal walk, starting from a small parking area at the end of the road. Cross the stile and follow the path which heads down to the beach and up the other side, then simply keep to the coastline past beaches of black boulders, with the imposing cliffs of Dore Holm soon coming into view. As you walk, it will soon become apparent that Dore Holm boasts an enormous arch, carved by the sea: walking to the end of the headland will give you a fine view of it. Continue around the cliff edge and begin ascending to a stone cross: from here, you could take the stile on your left to return to the start point, or follow the coastline for about four hundred metres further for splendid, front-on views of Dore Holm. Now either retrace your steps to the cross and take the path to the walk's beginning, or, if you're in the mood for a longer outing, you could continue from

Northmavine

ATLANTIC OCEAN

Quida Dale
Gluss Water
Whal Wick
HAMNAVOE
Grind o da Navir
Hamna Voe
Hole of Scraada
BORDIGARTH
Esha Ness
BRAEWICK
The Bruddans
NULLARBOR
TANGWICK
Brae Wick
Stenness
Tangwick Haa Museum
Tang Wick
The Neap
No Ness
Isle of Stenness

N

● SHOP	
Esme Wilcock Jewellery	1

■ ACCOMMODATION	
Braewick Caravan Park	1
St Magnus Bay Hotel	2

● RESTAURANTS AND CAFÉS	
Braewick Café	1
St Magnus Bay Hotel	2

0 — kilometres — 4
0 — miles — 2

89

NORTHMAVINE

Map of Northmavine, Shetland

Locations shown on the map:

- Isle of Fethaland
- Uyea Island
- North Wick
- Fethaland
- Grund Ness
- Fugla Ness
- SANDVOE
- ISBISTER
- South Wick
- Sandvoe
- Loch of Flugarth
- Potoz Plane
- Hevda Dale
- NORTH ROE
- Nort Trow Garden
- Moosa Water
- Burra Voe
- Muckle Holm
- Muckle Lunga Water
- Birka Water
- Sandy Water
- Roer Water
- Lang Ayre
- Roer Water
- Beorgs of Housetter
- HILLSIDE
- HOUSETTER
- NORTH SEA
- NORTH COLLAFIRTH
- Ronas Hill (1,480ft)
- Collafirth Hill (764ft)
- Ness of Queyfirth
- SOUTH COLLAFIRTH
- Quey Firth
- Loch of Queyfirth
- Lamba
- 380ft
- OLLABERRY
- White Grunafirth (567ft)
- HEYLOR
- Orr Wick
- SWINISTER
- Bay of Ollaberry
- Little Roe
- ASSATER
- Fann Hill (567ft)
- School
- Gluss Isle
- URAFIRTH
- Eela Water
- BURNSIDE
- Weaving Shed Gallery
- Hillswick Seal Sanctuary
- NORTH GLUSS
- Gluss Voe
- Calback Ness
- ss of swick
- Hillswick Circular
- MSHONADALE
- BARDISTER
- Hamar Voe
- Sullom Voe Oil Terminal
- Punds Water
- BURRALAND
- ENISFIRTH
- HOUBANS
- GUNNISTER
- Voe of Scatsta
- Vog Minn
- SULLOM
- Garths Voe
- NIBON
- Gunnister Man Stone
- Scatsta Ness
- Isle of Nibon
- LUNNISTER
- MANGASTER
- Loch of Lunnister
- HAGGRISTER
- Mainland
- Mangaster Voe
- Too Brekk
- Voxter Ness
- Eglisay
- Bight of Haggrister
- Dalescord Hill (826ft)
- South Sound
- Mavis Grind
- BRAE
- Ness of Houll

Esha Ness

the Dore Holm viewpoint along the coast to Tangwick.

Esha Ness
MAP PAGE 88
Off B9078, ZE2 9RS. Free.

Even among Shetland's typically stunning scenery, the coastal walk at Esha Ness stands out. Beginning at the squat white and yellow lighthouse – the last lighthouse to be designed by one of the prolific Stevenson family – take the path east along the gorgeously jagged cliffs, formed from dramatic volcanic activity some 395 million years ago.

The route follows the coast edge, threading inland periodically to allow you to walk around the deep canyons in the cliffs, known as geos. Try to stick near the edge as much as possible – the scenery has a raw, elemental beauty, and you don't want to miss the sight of the waves crashing over these rugged black rocks. That being said, take care – the cliffs are dangerous, especially in windy weather, and a misstep could be disastrous. This is not a walk for a day with poor visibility.

After passing a stretch of particularly dramatic coastline, you'll cross a ladder stile into a field. Here, follow the track that heads inland a little, and soon a large chasm will open up before you. This is the Hole of Scraada, a geo which is not yet fully formed: the sea has forced its way through the cliffs and created a tunnel, but the land overhead has not yet collapsed, thus giving you the bizarre spectacle of standing on an enormous land bridge looking down on the sea washing into the geo.

Along the right-hand side of Scraada are the ruins of an Iron Age broch, demonstrating that this rugged terrain has been inhabited for several thousand years. It sits peacefully in a picturesque spot on the edge of the Loch of Houlland.

Returning to the cliffs along the opposite side of Scraada, passing the waterfall that flows out of the loch, you can resume the main path and cross numerous stiles to the Grind o da Navir, a dramatic field of volcanic boulders strewn along the cliff. Overlooking a jagged bay of black rock, it's a marvellous testament to the power of nature.

From here, you can retrace your steps to Esha Ness Lighthouse, or – if you're hungry for more – you can continue, veering inland at Hamna Voe and circling round to Tangwick. You could even continue to Dore Holm and loop back to Esha Ness from Stenness, making a long but very satisfying circular walk.

Ollaberry
MAP PAGE 88
Off A970, Ollaberry, ZE2 9SA. Free.

Shetland offers plenty of fascinating geological features to discover, one of which can be found at Ollaberry. Here you can take a good look at the Walls Boundary Fault, a split in the Earth's crust which has resulted in major movement of rock over millions of years. Found at a small beach a short walk from Ollaberry Kirk, you can see where soft schist rock has eroded against hard granite, leaving a 20m-high wall of exposed granite. It is the best place in the UK to see an exposed fault of this type.

Ronas Hill
MAP PAGE 88
Off A970, Ronas Hill, ZE2 9RX. Free.
At just 450 metres tall, Ronas Hill doesn't trouble Scotland's big leagues, but it is the highest point on Shetland, and – if you're lucky enough to catch it on a clear day – the views from the summit are marvellous. As you climb, you'll see hardy Arctic plants and cross boulder fields formed by the effect of extreme cold and high winds. At the top, there's an ancient chambered cairn, constructed in Neolithic times.

The easiest way to climb it is from the car parking area next to the radio masts at the summit of Collafirth Hill, from which you can cross a plateau and begin an ascent – the out and back should take you about four hours. To make a real day of it, you can descend the western side of Ronas Hill to reach the extremely remote and beautiful sandy beach of Langayre. This is a lengthy outing in some of Shetland's wildest terrain, so make sure you go prepared for the weather to turn.

Beorgs of Housetter
MAP PAGE 88
A970, ZE2 9RZ. Free.
Between the villages of Housetter and North Roe, look for a small brown hut on the side of a loch to your right. Here, on the left of the road, is a pair of standing stones known as the Beorgs of Housetter. They're mossy and atmospheric, worth a quick two-minute tramp across the moorland to pay a visit.

Nort Trow Garden
MAP PAGE 88
North Haa Rd, North Roe, ZE2 9RY. Free, donations welcome.
A successful community project in North Roe has resulted in this delightful walled garden, which is immaculately kept and imaginatively designed. There's a pretty cottage garden, a vegetable plot, flowers planted in boats and sculpted earthworks, a rockery, and even a slightly unnerving totem pole.

The Potoz Plane
MAP PAGE 88
North Roe, ZE2 9RY. Free.
Aviation enthusiasts may want to make a quick stop in North Roe, where a small Potoz passenger plane sits, clearly visible from the road. The plane malfunctioned as it was landing at Sumburgh Airport in 1981, and though nobody was hurt as it skidded along the runway, the plane itself was a write-off. It sat at Sumburgh

Shetland Geopark

Shetland's geology is sufficiently impressive to warrant its designation as a UNESCO Geopark, recognising its outstanding geological heritage and sustainable development. As one of just two Geoparks in Scotland, Shetland is an extremely important site for geology enthusiasts, with seemingly endless remarkable formations to admire. Northmavine is a particularly significant area, with the Esha Ness peninsula alone boasting six especially important sites, and the Walls Boundary Fault at Ollaberry is also a site of major interest. Check out the Shetland Geopark website (www.shetland.org/geopark) to learn more.

View towards Fethaland

until 2005, when it was salvaged by Duncan Feather and brought to his house here. The project to restore it is ongoing. Visitors are welcome to walk up the track and examine the plane more closely.

Uyea Island
MAP PAGE 88
Off A970, ZE2 9RY. Free.

The island of Uyea, reached via a lengthy walk from Sandvoe near the village of North Voe, is a beautiful sight. Connected to the Mainland by a tombolo, the route to reach it offers gorgeously rugged coastal scenery and excellent wildlife spotting opportunities, as well as the chance to see some of Britain's oldest rocks here, approximately three billion years old. It also passes by the Beorgs of Uyea, a Neolithic-era quarry from which the raw material for felsite axes and knives was obtained. This is an all-day outing (allow at least seven hours), but a hugely rewarding hike.

Fethaland
MAP PAGE 88
Off A970, ZE2 9RY. Free.

The northernmost point of Northmavine is the peninsula of Fethaland, an exposed finger of land pointing north into the Atlantic Ocean. At the tip is a lighthouse, a worthwhile destination for a dramatic coastal walk of about 11 kilometres, which should take four hours or so.

The walk starts from the end of the road in Isbister: take the right-hand fork, heading uphill and passing the cemetery. The track becomes a rough path heading eastwards, passing through a gate and climbing slightly to a stile initially hidden behind a small rise. Cross the stile and press straight ahead, passing between ruined cottages on your left and the Loch of Houllsquey on the other side. After crossing another stile, turn left and follow the coastline, with views across to Yell on your right.

After several kilometres, the coast bends round to the left, and you'll be able to see Fethaland Lighthouse on the peninsula opposite. As you walk along the coast here, keep an eye out for seals in the inlets. When you reach the isthmus to Fethaland, you'll find the substantial ruins of a haaf fishing station, which was Shetland's busiest and most productive throughout the nineteenth century.

Cross the isthmus onto Fethaland and enjoy views of its jagged coast as you make your way up to the lighthouse. This is the furthest north you can go on Mainland, but across the sound you can see Yell and Unst stretching away still further north.

Crossing back across the causeway, the simplest route back initially follows the line of telegraph wires, but soon veers slightly right to pick up a roughly paved road, which leads back to Isbister. It's not the most exciting or picturesque of routes, though, and it involves some frankly unwelcome hills. An alternative, but considerably longer, route keeps to the western side of the peninsula and follows the coast down into the inlet of Sand Voe, from which you can cut inland to Isbister.

Shop

Esme Wilcock Jewellery
MAP PAGE 88
Hillswick, ZE2 9RW. http://facebook.com/esmemadebyshetland.
For some lovely handmade jewellery inspired by Shetland's natural landscapes, especially the sea, pay a visit to Esme Wilcock's workshop. Starting with sea glass and shells, Esme crafts beautiful pieces, and also runs silversmithing workshops for those keen to make their own jewellery.

Café

Braewick Café
MAP PAGE 88
B9078, Braewick, ZE2 9RS.
http://facebook.com/BraewickCafe.
With excellent views down into Braewick's bay, this welcoming café-restaurant is a splendid place for lunch on the Esha Ness peninsula. The menu changes periodically, but expect options such as macaroni cheese, burgers and spaghetti bolognaise. On Sundays, you may find a roast dinner available. ££

Restaurant

St Magnus Bay Hotel
MAP PAGE 88
Hillswick, ZE2 9RW.
http://stmagnusbayhotel.co.uk.
The restaurant of St Magnus Bay Hotel makes a fun attempt to take you back to the Viking era, with Norse shields and axes adorning the wood-panelled walls. It's a great atmosphere, and happily the food measures up: it's particularly good on local fish and seafood, but there are plenty of tasty meaty and vegetarian options available. £££

St Magnus Bay Hotel

Yell

Shetland's second-largest island, Yell sometimes seems to get a raw deal, often used simply as a bridge by travellers keen to press on to the more northerly island of Unst. That's a shame, as Yell has plenty to offer in its own right, including great coastal walks, an engaging museum, fascinating history, and a couple of Shetland's very best beaches. All in all, it's well worth spending a day or two exploring Yell, rather than hurrying straight through.

Catalina Memorial
MAP PAGE 96
Off B9081, ZE2 9BA. Free.

In 1942, an RAF Catalina aeroplane crashed on Yell, killing seven of its ten crew members. The crash site is now a memorial to the tragedy, with a cross erected and the remnants of the plane still in situ. It can be reached by following a farm track, and then white posts across the heather, from a small parking area near a bridge about a kilometre west of Hamnavoe.

St Magnus Church
MAP PAGE 96
B9081, ZE2 9BA.
http://scotlandschurchestrust.org.uk/church/st-magnus-hamnavoe-yell. Free.

The church of Hamnavoe village is a smart, grey-white building dating from 1838. The victims of the 1942 Catalina plane crash are buried in the churchyard, just to the right of the entrance gate. The church is often locked, but if it's open you can venture inside for a look at the tapestry woven by the pilot's widow.

St Colman's Church
MAP PAGE 96
Brunthill Rd, Burravoe, ZE2 9AY.
http://episcopalshetland.org.uk/st-colmans-burravoe. Free.

At the centre of Burravoe village, St Colman's Church – which is Scottish Episcopal, rather than the more usual Presbyterian – is one of the prettiest churches in Shetland. It's an elegant little stone building, with an attractive wooden beamed ceiling and understated but attractive stained glass in the windows. Though perhaps not worth a special trip, you could consider a quick stop en route to the Old Haa.

Getting to Yell

Ferries from the Mainland to Yell depart from Toft, with frequent departures on large ferries that can carry approximately 30 cars. With this capacity, you'll rarely have any issue getting a place on the Yell ferry, but it's still advisable to book, particularly if you're intending to continue on to Unst or Fetlar. The ferry takes about ten minutes and arrives at Ulsta, at which point the road splits almost immediately. The main road is the A968 which heads north along the west coast, while the more minor B9081 hugs the south and eastern coasts, eventually rejoining the A968 at Mid Yell. The majority of visitors will head straight up the A968 en route to the Unst ferry terminal at Gutcher, so if you're hoping to explore Yell consider first taking the B9081 to have the island to yourself.

The Old Haa Museum
MAP PAGE 96
Brough Rd, Burravoe, ZE2 9AY.
http://oldhaa.com. Free.

The Old Haa is a gorgeous white building which dates back to 1672, and now serves as Yell's museum. Before heading inside, check out the two memorials by the door: one is the propeller of the crashed Catalina aircraft, and the other is a sculpture dedicated to local naturalist Bobby Tulloch.

To the right as you enter is a wood-panelled room which explores the tragedy of the *Bohus*, a German vessel which ran aground off Yell in 1924. Exhibits consist of pieces salvaged from the vessel, including an intact and still undrunk bottle of whisky. You can also hear a radio interview with one of the survivors, recorded in 1989, detailing the events.

Head up the stairs to the gloriously uneven landing, and turn right into the "Sunday room", which is decorated as a smart reception room of centuries gone by, and also displays a range of historic artefacts discovered by local character Brucie Henderson, from Stone Age implements to eighteenth century coins. The final room covers natural history, of which the pride of the collection is the enormous jawbone of a sperm whale. There's also a display of local shells, and some engaging and informative boards covering Yell's geology.

Downstairs, the Old Haa also boasts a gift shop selling local knitwear, and a very welcome tearoom.

Gossabrough
MAP PAGE 96
Off B9081, ZE2 9AU. Free.

There are two reasons to visit the small settlement of Gossabrough. Archeology enthusiasts will be tempted here by the scant remains of an Iron Age broch, now not much more than a picturesque grassy mound, with the foundations of other buildings nearby. Sun worshippers, meanwhile, will enjoy the beach, which is a pretty sweep of fine white sand lapped by the dark sea.

The White Wife

The White Wife
MAP PAGE 96
Off B9081, ZE2 9AX. Free.

In 1924, the German vessel *Bohus*, en route from Gothenburg to Chile, found itself off course in the waters near Yell, and was grounded off the Ness of Queyon, near Otterswick. Four lives were lost, and it would likely have been more if not for the swift action taken by the local inhabitants in making rescue attempts. The figurehead of the *Bohus*, the White Wife, was set as a memorial to the tragedy on the shoreline near Otterswick, where it stood for nearly a century before being replaced with the current accurate replica. Staring out across the bay, it offers a sobering reminder of the dangers of the sea.

To reach the White Wife, follow the brown sign from the B9081 and drive to the end of the road, then continue on foot from the small parking area. A signpost

Yell

ATLANTIC OCEAN

ACCOMMODATION
Burravoe Caravan Site	2
Quam B&B	1

RESTAURANTS AND CAFÉS
Isle Eat	1
LJ's Diner	2
Old Haa Museum	3

SHOP
The Shetland Gallery	1

Outsta Ness
Breckon Sands
GLOUP
Gloup Fisherman's Memorial
Bay of Brough
BRECKON
Papil Bay
CULLIVOE
STONGANESS
Bluemull Sound
Unst
Belmont Ferry Terminal
Gutcher Ferry Terminal
Gossa Water
DALSETTER
GUTCHER
Linga
SELLAFIRTH
NORTH SANDWICK
Loch of Lumbister
Basta Voe
Broch of Burraness
Hamars Ness
BASTA
Sweinna Stack
EFSTIGARTH
Da Herra
GRIMISTER
RAGA
WINDHOUSE
CAMB
Hascosay
Mid Yell Voe
SETTER
MID YELL
South Sound
VATSETTER
WEST SANDWICK
Yell
Loch of Vatsetter
Yell Sound
AYWICK
Colgrave Sound
OTTERS WICK
The White Wife
▲ Hill of Noub (505ft)
▲ Hill of Arisdale (688ft)
WEST YELL
Ness of Sound
GOSSABROUGH
Brother
Uynarey
Catalina Memorial
Loch of Kettlester
St Magnus Church
HAMNAVOE
BURRAVOE
St. Colman's Church
Old Haa Museum
ULSTA
Ulsta Ferry Terminal
COPISTER
Bigga
Wick of Copister
N
Mainland
Toft Ferry Terminal
Samphrey
Orfasay

| 0 | kilometres | 3 |
| 0 | miles | 2 |

guides you through a gate and across a couple of fields, heading towards a ruined stone structure. From this, you can see the White Wife standing on the shoreline below. A path continues around the cliffs from the White Wife to Aywick, which makes for a delightful coastal walk.

Mid Yell
MAP PAGE 96
B9081, ZE2 9BN. Free.
Mid Yell is the largest village on Yell, and is where you'll find many of the island's services, including a shop, café and a small restaurant. It's therefore worth a quick stop, particularly around lunchtime.

Ness of Sound
MAP PAGE 96
Off A968, ZE2 9BG. Free.
The A968, which heads up Yell's west coast from the ferry terminal, is a very scenic road, offering fantastic views across to North Mainland. A particularly fine viewpoint can be found above the Ness of Sound, a pretty little green island connected to Yell by a small causeway. It's similar to St Ninian's Isle (see page 46), with the sea lapping beaches on both sides of the causeway.

West Sandwick
MAP PAGE 96
Off A968, ZE2 9BH. Free.
The little beach at West Sandwick has to be one of Shetland's best, with its lovely yellow sand, picturesque rocks at either end of the bay, and superb views out to sea, with numerous little islands dotting the water as you gaze across to North Mainland. It's a very fine place to enjoy a sunny day.

Da Herra
MAP PAGE 96
Off A968, ZE2 9BL. Free.
Da Herra, the peninsula just north of West Sandwick is relatively wild country, which is suited for some lengthy walks for adventurous types, rewarded with views over the impressive sea stacks that can be seen just off the shore here: the Stacks of Stuis are reasonably easy to reach, while the Ern Stack will require a bit more of a walk. In the heart of the headland, and accessible by car, is a memorial to the local musician Peerie Willie Johnson, who grew up on Yell – indeed, his former home can be seen across the valley from the memorial.

The Windhouse
MAP PAGE 96
Off A968, ZE2 9BJ. Free.
On the hill above the A968 just after you pass Da Herra is a ruined grey stone building known as the Windhouse. It was an eighteenth-century laird's house, and is thought to have been built on the site of a medieval graveyard, which has contributed to its reputation as Shetland's most haunted building. It certainly looks appropriately creepy, and should you wish to go ghost-hunting, you can make your way up to it to explore.

The Broch of Burraness
MAP PAGE 96
Off A968, ZE2 9DF. Free.
The Broch of Burraness is one of Shetland's best-preserved brochs, although this isn't immediately apparent on approaching it, as from the landward side it looks like a simple mound. Walking to the side facing the sea, however, reveals the impressive round walls, now draped in moss and lichen. Imagining it at its likely full height – about nine metres – gives an idea of how imposing it must have been, guarding this stretch of water between Yell and Fetlar. Other mounds in the earth here suggest further remains; it's likely this was once a thriving community.

Reaching the broch requires a roughly 90 minute out-and-back walk, which can be done from North Sandwick or Kirkabister, though the North Sandwick route

Haaf fishing

During the eighteenth and nineteenth centuries, many men in Shetland were engaged in haaf fishing, a low-paid and dangerous job which was often the only employment option available. In six-oared boats known as sixareens, groups of fishermen would row up to 40 miles offshore where they would set their lines and hope to come back laden with fish. Their catches were returned to haaf stations, which were found around Shetland: the remains of one of the largest can still be seen at Fethaland, in Northmavine. At these stations the fish was cured and prepared for export. The fishermen saw very little profit from their expeditions, due to the 'truck' system in operation, which required fishermen to pay the local laird for the use of the boat and accommodation at the haaf station. Improvements in labour laws, as well as the Gloup disaster, contributed to the demise of haaf fishing, but it was largely the development of the larger and more efficient steam trawler – which could easily outfish a group of fishermen in sixareens – that brought the haaf system to an end.

is the more picturesque. Starting from the gate at the end of the North Sandwick road, take the stile and head down towards the small beach, passing through a couple of rickety gates. Cross the stream on the beach and then pass beside the ruined house, after which you need only stick to the coastline following the row of guideposts until you cross a metal stile. From here, the guideposts give out, but just keep to the cliffs and you'll soon descend to a long stony beach, backed by a small loch. The broch is now within sight at the other end of the beach's peninsula: simply walk towards it.

Gutcher
MAP PAGE 96
A968, ZE2 9DF. Free.
Gutcher probably holds the record as Yell's most visited destination – it's the ferry terminal to Unst and Fetlar. From here, the B9082 leads further into Yell's northern reaches.

Cullivoe
MAP PAGE 96
B9082, ZE2 9DD. Free.
The village of Cullivoe is particularly worth visiting between May and August, when its Galley Shed exhibition on the island's Up Helly Aa festival is open. Otherwise, you may still want to visit to pick up a boat trip from the pier, especially if you're keen on going sea fishing.

Breckon Sands
MAP PAGE 96
Off B9083, ZE2 9DD. Free.
Breckon Sands is an absolutely perfect beach, a lovely sweep of yellow-white sand backed by grassy dunes, and with great waves rolling in from the ocean – gazing out to sea here, there's nothing between you and the Faroe Islands, more than 300 kilometres away. If you catch the beach on a warm and sunny day, it's a sensational place.

For those in the mood for exploring, a very worthwhile path leads along the back of the sand dunes and out onto the little peninsula to the beach's east. This walk, which also includes passing by a wild and stony beach, takes you past a couple of rectangular arrangements of stones. Although there have been no formal archeological studies, these are thought to be all that remains of Viking longhouses.

Gloup Fishermen's Memorial

MAP PAGE 96
Off B9083, ZE2 9DD. Free.

On the cliffs by the small settlement of Gloup is a simple, affecting memorial to the 58 local men who lost their lives in 1881 when a storm blew up as they were out haaf fishing. Such an enormous loss of life was devastating for the local communities, and the disaster may have contributed to the decline in use of the traditional Shetland sixareen boats.

From the memorial, you can begin a lengthy walk which follows the line of the coast down Gloup Voe, then up the other side to reach the Holm of Gloup – where you stand a good chance of spotting seals – and further to the Iron Age fort at Burgi Stack.

Breckon Sands

Shop

The Shetland Gallery

MAP PAGE 96
Sellafirth, ZE2 9DG.
http://shetlandgallery.com.

This friendly art gallery contains original pictures by artists from all over Shetland, all available for purchase. Also on sale are pieces of jewellery by local artisans. It's a great place to pick up an evocative souvenir.

Restaurant

LJ's Diner

MAP PAGE 96
Mid Yell, ZE2 9BN.
http://facebook.com/midyell.

At time of writing, LJ's Diner was closed and not expecting to reopen until 2025. Hopefully it does so, because it's the only place on Yell that reliably served hot meals: think burgers, pizzas and the like. Check its Facebook page for updates. ££

Cafés

Isle Eat

MAP PAGE 96
Mid Yell, ZE2 9BJ. 01957 702071.

The small café attached to Mid Yell's Hillshop convenience store keeps very irregular hours (usually Friday and Saturday only, if that), but if you do find it open, you can enjoy excellent breakfasts and simple lunches. Don't rely on it, but treat it as a bonus if it's serving. £

The Old Haa Tearoom

MAP PAGE 96
Brough Rd, Burravoe, ZE2 9AY.
http://oldhaa.com.

Located in the Old Haa Museum, this cosy little tearoom offers good coffee and a selection of tasty fancies (cakes) – the ginger cake is deliciously fiery. It's also an excellent spot to get up-to-date information on current affairs on Yell and recommendations for activities. £

Fetlar

Fetlar describes itself as the Garden of Shetland, and your first impression on getting off the ferry is likely to be that it is indeed very green. Although it's Shetland's fourth largest island, the population is very low, partly as a result of the croft clearances in the nineteenth century and partly due to high emigration in the 1950s. It has a long history, extending back at least 5,500 years, at which time a large wall known as Finnigert Daek was constructed, dividing the island from north to south, for reasons unknown. There's little to see of Finngert Daek now, but visitors can explore other historical sites, both ancient and modern, from the Viking-era Giant's Grave to the eighteenth-century Brough Lodge, as well as taking the opportunity to spot some of Shetland's rarest birds.

Brough Lodge

MAP PAGE 101
Off B9088, ZE2 9DJ.
http://europeanheritageproject.com/brough-lodge. Free.

On Fetlar's west coast you'll find the ruins of the grand Brough Lodge, once home to the notorious Sir Arthur Nicolson, who in the eighteenth century evicted many tenants from their holdings on Fetlar so he could use the land for sheep farming. He built himself this Gothic castle-like home to live in, complete with a distinctive tower, on the site of a former broch. Unfortunately, the house is not open to the public, though it can be seen easily from the roadside – you can't miss the tower from the main road, though to get a look at the house itself you'll need to take the side road down to Brough Pier. To see the interior, you can either check out the photo display at the Fetlar Interpretative Centre, or wait until the Lodge's planned renovation is complete: there are allegedly plans to convert it into a luxury hotel.

Haltadans Stone Circle

MAP PAGE 101
Off B9088, ZE2 9DJ. Free.

This remnant of Fetlar's ancient past can be found by following a path from the island's disused airstrip. The story goes that the stones were once trolls dancing in a circle before the sunlight turned them to stone. There are more impressive sights to seek out on Fetlar, but if you're a stone circle enthusiast or have plenty of time on your hands, they're just about worth the walk.

Getting to Fetlar

Regular, if not particularly frequent (four or five daily), ferries to Hamars Ness on Fetlar leave from Gutcher on Yell and Belmont on Unst. The ferry takes cars and foot passengers. If you're taking your car to Fetlar, it's advisable to book the ferry in advance to ensure you get a spot: it's rarely busy, but if by chance there's not enough room for you, you'll be looking at a long wait for the next one.

Tresta Beach

MAP PAGE 101
Off B9088, ZE2 9DJ. Free.

Tresta Beach is a lovely sandy beach on Fetlar's south coast. Access is from the austere Fetlar Kirk, and you'll walk down along a causeway separating the beach from the loch of Papil Water, a good spot for trout fishing as well as a popular hangout for great skuas. The beach itself is a wide expanse of sand and shingle in an enclosed bay, protected to the south by the imposing mass of Lamb Hoga. A walk starts here which ascends the obvious track onto the top of Lamb Hoga, taking you past peat bogs which were historically cut by Fetlar's islanders.

Houbie

MAP PAGE 101
B9088, ZE2 9DJ. Free.

The little village of Houbie is Fetlar's principal settlement. It's a

Brough Lodge

small place, but boasts a shop and café, the island's museum, a small beach and a smattering of self-catering accommodation. The large white house at the village's eastern end is Leagarth House, once home to Sir William Watson Cheyne, who assisted Lord Lister in the development of antiseptic surgery. The Fetlar Interpretive Centre has an award-winning display on Sir William's life.

Fetlar Interpretative Centre
MAP PAGE 101
B9088, ZE2 9DJ.
http://fetlar.org/things/activities/fetlar-interpretive-centre. Charge.

The excellent Fetlar Interpretative Centre has a fine collection of displays on island-related topics, including a fascinating history of Brough Lodge, examples of Fetlar knitwear, an engaging run-through of local folklore (with marvellously dry feminist undertones), and some archeological artefacts from the Stone Age and Norse eras. Add to that some very good collections and information on Fetlar's past fishing industry and interesting biographies of the island's historical characters – including Sir William Watson Cheyne – and all in all you've got one of Shetland's best local museums.

Aith
MAP PAGE 101
B9088, ZE2 9DJ. Free.

The small stony beach at Aith had long been the subject of local legend, maintaining that after a fierce storm, a Viking laden with treasure had been buried here, along with his boat. A *Time Team* excavation in 2002 suggested there was some truth to the story – there was certainly a grave here, though it had been robbed of almost all the legendary treasure. An exquisite brooch, however, was found, as well as a large soapstone bowl, both of which are now on show in the Shetland Museum in Lerwick.

Loch of Funzie
MAP PAGE 101
B9088, ZE2 9DJ. Free.

Popular with anglers keen to enjoy trout angling, the Loch of Funzie is also a good spot for birdwatching – there's an RSPB hide here for spotting Fetlar's population of

Walking to the Gruting folly

To reach the folly, take the road to Kirkhouse, and at the end of the road follow the footpath signpost onto an easy track. As the track bends to the right, cut across the grass toward a stile directly ahead. Cross it, then pass some ruined cottages and keep close to the wall on your right until you descend to a burn. Here, take the gate into the next (often boggy) field, cross the burn, and continue with the wall on your left to a ladder stile. Crossing this brings you onto a clear track leading ahead and slightly right, until it bends left at the top of a rise. Leave the track here and descend the slope, making for a metal stile in the fence opposite. The folly is now directly ahead – simply climb up to it. It's enclosed by a wall: the entranceway is on the left.

Make it a circular walk by following the track from the folly towards the sea, staying atop the rise until you see a stile below you on the right. Descend towards it, cross, and follow the shoreline back, ascending to a metal stile and following a fence line. The beach here is Gruting Bay, which according to tradition is the first place the Vikings landed on Shetland. After crossing a little stream, cut uphill and aim for the field wall to rejoin your outward path. Allow about an hour and a half for the round trip.

Fetlar Interpretative Centre

rare red-necked phalaropes and whimbrel. On the loch's shore is a large stone model which looks a little like the Loch Ness Monster: check out the information board to see how it demonstrates the geological forces that formed the rocks of Fetlar.

Gruting
MAP PAGE 101
Off B9088, ZE2 9DJ. Free.
Not content with building the massive Brough Lodge on the west side of Fetlar, Sir Arthur Nicolson also constructed a folly in the northeast. It's ruined and overgrown now, but the tall circular walls of the tower remain, adorned with slightly pretentious Greek columns. Having been built with stone from the houses of evicted crofters, the tower is reputed to be haunted.

Funzie and the Snap
MAP PAGE 101
Off B9088, ZE2 9DJ. Free.
Okay, 'Funzie and the Snap' might sound like a subpar noughties indie band, but it's actually an excellent, well-signposted walk in Fetlar's southeast. Starting from the stony Funzie Beach, it heads three kilometres around the coast to the headland known as the Snap, passing some gorgeous rugged scenery as it goes. This is a perfect walk for spotting seabirds, with the cliffs here ideal nesting territory for skuas and fulmars, among others. Beware during the nesting season in the spring, though: some of the residents may feel threatened and resort to dive-bombing you.

Café

Fetlar Café
MAP PAGE 101
Houbie, B9088, ZE2 9DJ. 01957 733227.
This welcome little café attached to Houbie's village shop offers a short menu of good lunch options: soups, sandwiches and filled rolls. There are also some good cakes, and tea and coffee. It's the only eating option on Fetlar, so it's lucky that it's good. £

Unst

You'll hear a lot of 'most northerly's on Unst – it's the UK's most northerly inhabited island, which means that there are plenty of facilities and attractions that are also the most northerly: the most northerly pub, shop, post box, lighthouse, to name a very few. But even without these superlatives, Unst is more than worth a visit: among much else, it boasts gorgeous beaches, Viking longhouses, Iron Age brochs, a spaceport and Britain's most celebrated bus stop. Although a day trip from Mainland is plausible, you'll need a minimum of two days to get the most out of a visit to Unst.

Belmont Longhouse
MAP PAGE 106
Off A968, ZE2 9DW. Free.
Unst is famous for its Viking longhouses – it has the greatest concentration of them in Europe – so it's no surprise that you'll come across one pretty much as soon as you're off the ferry. Signposted off the road to the right as you head northward, it's a fairly typical example of the Viking homestead style.

Uyeasound
MAP PAGE 106
Uyeasound, ZE2 9DW. Free.
The main settlement on the south coast of Unst, Uyeasound is an attractive little place. The village centre is at the pier, where you'll find its oldest buildings, which include Greenwell's Bod. This stolid square building dates back to the seventeenth century, and was likely used as a combination of warehouse and shop. It fell out of use at some point in the nineteenth century and is now in a state of ruin.

Clivocast Standing Stone
MAP PAGE 106
Clivocast, ZE2 9DL. Free.
The lichen-covered standing stone at Clivocast is in a field just beside the road. It's an impressively tall piece of rock, several metres in height, said to mark the spot where one of the sons of the Norwegian king Harald Fairhair was killed. In the year 875, Harald brought Shetland and Orkney under Norwegian overlordship, and is thought to have made landfall at Haroldswick in Unst. The death of his son here

Getting to Unst

Reaching Unst from the Mainland requires a ferry from Toft to Ulsta on Yell, then a drive across Yell to Gutcher, from which you can pick up a further ferry to Belmont on Unst. Note that the ferries plying the Gutcher to Belmont route are smaller than those operating between Toft and Ulsta, which means that if you're visiting on a busy day you could be left waiting at Gutcher. Booking in advance is therefore recommended. It takes approximately 30 minutes to drive from Ulsta to Gutcher, so make sure you leave sufficient time to get between them when booking your ferry. The crossing to Unst takes about ten minutes.

Longhouses

Longhouses are a traditional Norse construction, brought by Viking settlers to Shetland from around the eighth century onward. They varied in complexity and size, but essentially lived up to their name – they were long buildings divided into two or more rooms, one of which was a central living area while the others would house livestock or be used as a workshop. In Scandinavia, longhouses were often made of wood, but the limited supply of wood on Shetland meant that many were constructed from stone. Ruins of longhouses can be seen all over Unst, with particularly impressive examples at Underhoull and Sandwick, and there's also a reconstructed one at Haroldswick, which gives you the chance to see what these buildings may have looked like in their heyday.

may have been during a battle for control of the island.

Muness Castle

MAP PAGE 106
East of Clivocast, ZE2 9DL.
http://historicenvironment.scot/visit-a-place/places/muness-castle. Free.

An imposing sixteenth-century fortress built by the tyrannical Laurence Bruce, the dour Muness Castle boasts towers and elaborately designed turrets, as well as an impressive carved inscription above its entrance. The massive wooden door creaks satisfyingly as you push it open. You'll need a torch to explore the dark passageways on the lower level, but heading up the stairs to the right of the entrance will bring you to the main hall, now open to the elements but plainly a room built to impress. Be sure to step into the towers at either end of the upper floor: there are all-encompassing views from their windows, but the multiple gun holes rather suggest that Bruce did not expect friendly visitors.

Uyeasound

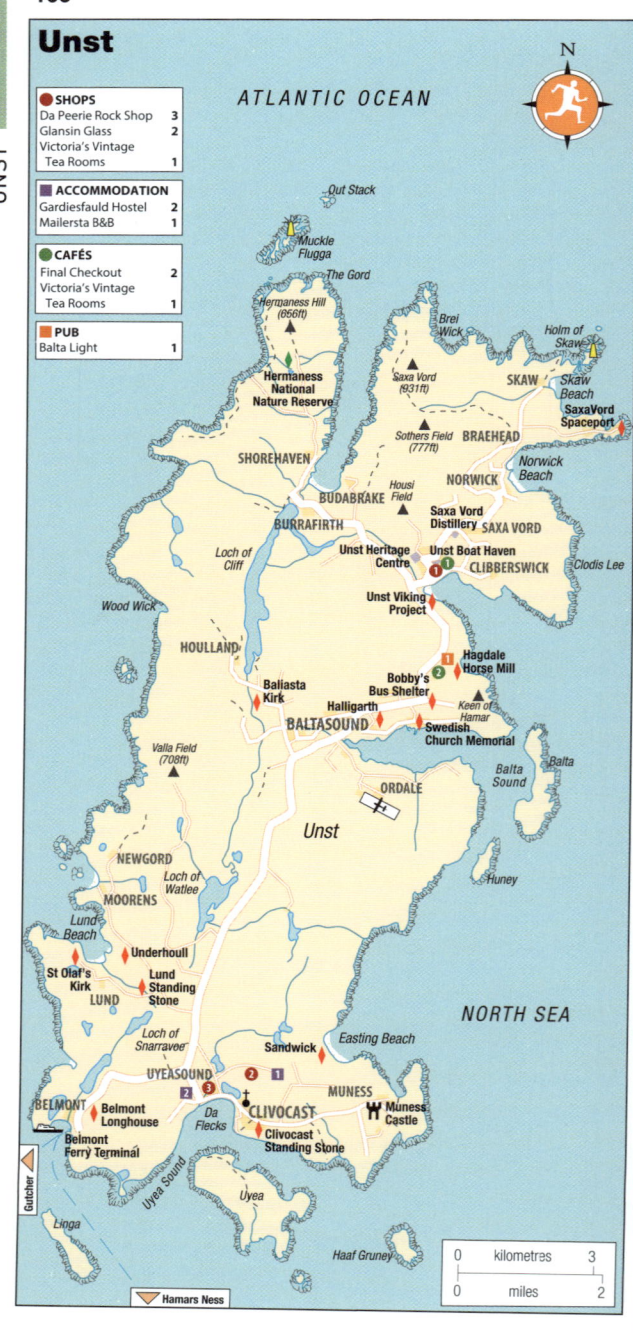

Unst

● **SHOPS**	
Da Peerie Rock Shop	3
Glansin Glass	2
Victoria's Vintage Tea Rooms	1

■ **ACCOMMODATION**	
Gardiesfauld Hostel	2
Mailersta B&B	1

● **CAFÉS**	
Final Checkout	2
Victoria's Vintage Tea Rooms	1

■ **PUB**	
Balta Light	1

Laurence Bruce

Laurence Bruce – a descendant of Robert the Bruce – became the sheriff of Shetland in the 1570s, and seems to have quickly set about exploiting his position to enrich himself, becoming notorious for his oppression of the local people. A royal commission in 1577 into his excesses resulted in his brief removal from office, but he was reappointed under a different title the following year. He built Muness Castle after falling out with his master, the similarly tyrannical Earl Patrick Stewart of Orkney, who briefly besieged the fortress in 1608. Bruce survived the assault and went on to denounce the Earl, who was summoned before Scotland's Privy Council to answer for his misgovernment of Orkney. After Stewart's subsequent rebellion and execution, Bruce retained royal favour and died at Muness in 1617.

Sandwick

MAP PAGE 106
Sandwick, ZE2 9DL. Free.

The pretty beach of Sandwick – sometimes called the Eastings – is well worth a stop for its attractive sweep of white sand, but it's also an important archeological site, where traces of settlement dating back to the Iron Age can be seen. The most impressive of these are the fairly substantial remains of a Viking longhouse, which is found almost on the beach in an area of grassy dunes just after you cross a stream.

Traces of Norse era settlement can be seen if you leave the beach at the northern end and follow the coast. In an enclosed cemetery, just before you reach a wall, is a ruined twelfth-century chapel; the bumps in the earth all round here are the remains of a large farm known as Framgord.

Lund Standing Stone

MAP PAGE 106
Lund, ZE2 9DW. Free.

Over towards the west coast, Shetland's largest standing stone is an impressively hefty chunk of rock, somewhat resembling an enormous shark's tooth jutting out of the earth. Erected perhaps as far back as the Neolithic period, its intended function is not known.

St Olaf's Kirk

MAP PAGE 106
Lund, ZE2 9DW. Free.

The picturesque ruins of the twelfth-century St Olaf's Kirk stand on the cliffside overlooking the pretty white sands of Lund Beach. As you head down to the church along the track from the parking area, in a field to your right you can seek out some earthworks showing the foundations of some Viking longhouses. From the church, you can pick up a path leading past the Loch of Snabrugh to the ferry at Belmont.

The Lund Standing Stone

Bobby's Bus Shelter

Underhoull
MAP PAGE 106
Lund, ZE2 9DW. Free.
A treat for archeology enthusiasts, the headland at Underhoull boasts the remains of several Viking longhouses as well as an Iron Age broch. The first longhouse is found about 50 metres from the road, its foundations clear to see; it was a large building, with several rooms of differing functions.

Continuing along the track from the information board, you'll quickly reach the remains of the broch. Although it now consists of grassy earthworks, it was clearly an impressive structure with fine views of this stretch of coastline. From the top of the broch, looking southwest you can see Lund Beach and St Olaf's Kirk and, more immediately, on the hillside below, the second longhouse.

Cross the stile and head steeply downhill, passing the remains of another Iron Age construction en route. The lower longhouse was a substantial building, with two sizeable rooms and other adjacent buildings. The occupants are thought to have been reliant on farming and fishing, making use of the land and sea in equal measure. You can continue along the coastline from here to Lund Beach and St Olaf's Kirk.

Baltasound
MAP PAGE 106
Baltasound, ZE2 9DS. Free.
The village of Baltasound is Unst's largest settlement and, though there's evidence of habitation dating back at least as far as the Viking era, it came to prominence during the Victorian period when it became a major centre for the herring fishing industry. It's home to several of the island's sights, including Bobby's famous bus shelter (see below), as well as amenities including a shop, café and pub.

Halligarth
MAP PAGE 106
Baltasound, ZE2 9DR. Free.
In the centre of Baltasound stands Halligarth, the former home of the local gentry, the Saxbys and Edmondstons. It's now empty and abandoned, but it's clear that it was once a fine house, with large gardens stretching down toward

the sea. Unusually for Unst, there's a copse of woodland here, which you can wander through to find the family's private graveyard.

Bobby's Bus Shelter
MAP PAGE 106
Baltasound, ZE2 9TW. Free.

Where the A968 bends round to the left is one of Shetland's quirkiest attractions: Bobby's Bus Shelter, which is seasonally decorated with a new theme every year. It's named after Bobby Macaulay, a seven-year-old who wrote to the local council after plans to remove the shelter were made. On Bobby's request, the shelter was not only saved, but given a full makeover and even contains a sofa and television. It was damaged in a car accident in September 2024, and at time of writing was undergoing a thorough renovation.

A few metres away, along the road to the Keen of Hamar, is a memorial plaque to the HMS *E-49*, a submarine which sank in the waters nearby during World War I after it hit a German mine. Thirty-one crew members lost their lives.

The Keen of Hamar
MAP PAGE 106
Baltasound, ZE2 9TW. http://nature.scot/enjoying-outdoors/visit-our-nature-reserves/keen-hamar-nature-reserve. Free.

One for botany enthusiasts, the Keen of Hamar has been designated a Site of Special Scientific Interest due to its being home to a variety of small and uncommon flowers. The rarest of these is Edmondston's chickweed, but the northern rock cress and Norwegian sandwort aren't far behind. Being small, though, they aren't easy to spot; you'll need to get close to the floor to take a look. This headland also contains the remains of a Viking longhouse which you can seek out on a circular walk from the car park.

Swedish Church Memorial
MAP PAGE 106
Baltasound, ZE2 9DS. Free.

Down near the pier, you'll find a stone marking the site of a church that was erected by Swedish fishermen who visited Baltasound in the early twentieth century. The church remained in use for several years, but after the fishermen stopped making the journey, it was used instead to house old boats. When the church eventually blew down in 1992, the boats were transferred to the Unst Boat Haven.

Baliasta Kirk
MAP PAGE 106
Baltasound, ZE2 9DZ. Free.

On the outskirts of Baltasound is the ruined church of Baliasta, now roofless and overgrown with ivy. It's particularly picturesque in the evening sunlight with the well-kept cemetery surrounding it.

The Edmondstons

During the nineteenth century, from their home at Halligarth, the Edmondston family became prominent naturalists. Laurence Edmondston was responsible for establishing the woodland on the Halligarth estate, and specialised in the description of birds native to the island, while his son Thomas was an accomplished botanist, discovering the rare flower Shetland mouse-ear – also known as Edmondston's chickweed – growing on the nearby Keen of Hamar. Laurence's daughter Jessie, meanwhile, married the ornithologist and doctor Henry Saxby, and became a successful writer, with output varying from local folklore collections to boys' adventure stories.

Hagdale Horse Mill

MAP PAGE 106
Baltasound, ZE2 9DS. Free.
Reached about five minutes along a path starting from the Balta Light pub, the horse mill is a fascinating remnant of the industrial age. Hagdale is home to the only major deposit of chromite – used for making paints and dyes – in the UK, and in the 1800s it was quarried here. This circular mill used horsepower to separate the chromite from heavier, less valuable, rocks. It still contains the large central wheel in its original position, with the now detached stone weight leaning against one of the walls.

Haroldswick

MAP PAGE 106
Haroldswick, ZE2 9ED. Free.
Named for the Norwegian King Harald Fairhair, the small settlement of Haroldswick is home to Unst's collection of three museums – the Unst Viking Project, Unst Boat Haven and Unst Heritage Centre – as well as a tearoom which makes one of the island's best places to stop for lunch.

Unst Boat Haven

Unst Viking Project

MAP PAGE 106
Haroldswick, ZE2 9ED. http://shetland amenity.org/viking-unst. Free.
The Unst Viking Project seeks to bring the Viking era back to life with the construction of a replica longhouse and ship. The longhouse is an amalgam of various longhouse designs, with stone walls and an authentic turf roof supported by wooden beams. Inside, you can easily imagine a fire in the hearth creating a cosy, if smoky, atmosphere. Beyond the longhouse is the replica ship, a magnificent craft with an exquisitely carved prow. It is an accurate reproduction of a ninth-century vessel that was discovered in Norway in 1880, and its builders originally intended to sail it to America. You can clamber aboard and picture yourself exploring the seas between Scandinavia and Shetland.

Unst Boat Haven

MAP PAGE 106
Beach Rd, Haroldswick, ZE2 9ED. http://unst heritage.co.uk/boat-haven. Charge.
The Unst Boat Haven consists of a large room in which are displayed fifteen historic boats gathered from around the island, as well as information boards covering a diverse range of topics, all pertaining to the sea and the islanders' relationship to it. The display of antique sailing equipment is fascinating, while kids are likely to be drawn to the fantastic model ships.

Unst Heritage Centre

MAP PAGE 106
Haroldswick, ZE2 9EE. http://unstheritage. co.uk/heritage-centre. Charge.
Unst Heritage Centre offers an excellent look at the island's history, culture and geology, presented largely chronologically. Beginning with Unst's geological formation, the main room progresses through displays of prehistoric artefacts, before reaching the Viking and Norse periods, and then the world wars, coming right up to date with

'Most northerly' in Haroldswick

Besides its museums and distillery, Haroldswick is a good place to visit if you're a 'most northerly' hunter: it's home to the UK's most northerly church and the most northerly post box. The former is a more worthwhile stop: the pebbledash walls outside hide a very pleasing interior, composed of wooden beams which bring to mind ships and Viking longhouses.

the development of the SaxaVord Spaceport. There are also displays on the Muckle Flugga Lighthouse and the diverse wildlife that can be seen around the island, with a special focus on Shetland ponies.

The second room contains excellent ethnographic displays on the life of nineteenth- and twentieth-century crofters, with reconstructions of rooms in croft houses containing plenty of artefacts – look out for the beautifully carved spinning chair and the ingenious expandable baby cradle.

Saxa Vord Distillery

MAP PAGE 106
Haroldswick, ZE2 9EF.
http://shetlandreel.com. Charge.

The UK's northernmost distillery produces award-winning gins to a variety of recipe, including Ocean Sent, inspired by the seas around Unst. You can enjoy a tour – including tastings, of course – of the distillery, though make sure to book in advance.

Hermanness Nature Reserve

MAP PAGE 106
Off B9086, ZE2 9EQ. http://nature.scot/enjoying-outdoors/visit-our-nature-reserves/hermaness-national-nature-reserve. Free.

The peninsula in Unst's northwest consists of the Hermanness Nature Reserve, a splendid place to spot seabirds, from gannets and kittiwakes to puffins and skuas. There are two established walking trails on the peninsula. The Muckle Flugga trail, which offers a circular route taking in excellent views of the Muckle Flugga Lighthouse, should take you between three and four hours. The shorter Saito trail, meanwhile, offers spectacular views of the peninsula's west coast, and takes about ninety minutes. Both initially follow the same route from the car park along an excellent wooden boardwalk, which ends when you reach the western cliffs; hereafter, whichever route you take, be prepared for the path to be boggy underfoot.

Saxa Vord

MAP PAGE 106
Off B9086, ZE2 9EQ. Free.

The highest point on Unst, the summit of Saxa Vord is home to an RAF listening post which is off-limits to casual visitors, but just outside the base's entrance is a bench offering stunning views across to Hermanness. You'll also find a Wild Skies information point here, covering the Northern Lights, which you may see at night from this vantage point.

A couple of hundred metres before you reach the base's entrance is a small parking area at which the Wild Skies Planetary Trail begins. This 1.5-kilometre route offers walkers the chance to explore the solar system without, as the sign helpfully notes, having to walk 4.5 billion kilometres. Each sign along the gentle trail gives information about the planets, accompanied by artwork by local residents and organisations. The views across to the opposite peninsula are superb, and if you're not down for the lengthy walk on Hermanness, the planetary trail offers your best view of Muckle Flugga.

The Wild Skies Trail

An excellent way to explore Unst is to follow the Wild Skies Trail (www.wildskiesshetland.com), a fantastic initiative which has set up interactive information panels at thirteen of Unst's top sights, including the Viking Project, Hermanness and Muness. These panels each take a different approach to looking at the skies of Unst – the board at the Keen of Hamar, for example, considers the solstice, while the one at the Viking Project investigates how the Vikings navigated using the stars. Many of the boards also have a listening post, with audio ranging from traditional music to oral history recorded by locals. Following the trail will lead you to many of Unst's highlights, and give you an insight into aspects of the island you may not otherwise have considered.

Norwick Beach
MAP PAGE 106
Norwick, ZE2 9EF. Free.

The glorious Norwick Beach is a wide expanse of yellow sand, backed by grassy dunes. The waves roar in, breaking against the small islet, known as the Taing, that stands in the centre of the beach: the waters are calmer to the left of this islet, should you be contemplating a dip. It's an absolutely beautiful place, which you're likely to have all to yourself even on a sunny day.

Norwick Beach

SaxaVord Spaceport
MAP PAGE 106
Lamba Ness, ZE2 9TJ. http://saxavord.com. Free.

It may come as something of a surprise to find a spaceport on Unst, but believe it or not, this is the facility from which the UK intends to launch many of its rockets once it becomes operational. In development since 2021 on the site of an old RAF listening post, once the spaceport is in use it is expected to see approximately 30 launches a year. Although you can take a look at the spaceport construction site from the road, don't trespass: signs warn that unauthorised visitors may be transported to Mars.

Skaw Beach
MAP PAGE 106
Skaw, ZE2 9EF. Free.

The very pretty Skaw Beach offers a small bay enclosed by low rocky cliffs, with a sweep of coarse yellow sand washed by an often wild sea. It's one of the very few beaches in the UK from which you can potentially see a rocket launch, once the nearby spaceport goes into operation. Rather more down-to-earth distinctions include the fact that this is the UK's most northerly sandy beach, the most northerly point of the UK National Cycle Route 1, and that the adjacent farm is the UK's most northerly occupied house.

Shops

Da Peerie Rock Shop

MAP PAGE 106
East Rd, Uyeasound, ZE2 9DN.
On Uyeasound's pier you'll find an honesty box shop where you can buy a pick and mix of brightly coloured rocks and crystals, ranging from lumps of rose quartz to pieces of lapis lazuli. Next door is Le Petit Café, also an honesty box system, which sells coffee, tea, and a selection of French cakes and biscuits.

Glansin Glass

MAP PAGE 106
Uyeasound, ZE2 9DL.
http://glansinglass.co.uk.
This small studio creates lovely glass souvenirs inspired by Shetland – there are pieces which evoke the ocean, others which use patterns suggesting the lace industry, and still more with a very contemporary feel. As well as buying ready-made works, you can also take classes to design and make your own.

Victoria's Vintage Tea Rooms

MAP PAGE 106
Beach Rd, Haroldswick, ZE2 9DU.
http://victoriasvintagetearooms.co.uk.
Attached to the tearoom is a great little shop selling all manner of Shetland- and Unst-themed souvenirs from tea towels and mugs to a small selection of knitwear.

Da Peerie Rock Shop

Victoria's Vintage Tea Rooms

MAP PAGE 106
Beach Rd, Haroldswick, ZE2 9DU.
http://victoriasvintagetearooms.co.uk.
Right on the waterfront in Haroldswick, Victoria's Vintage Tea Rooms is one of the best places on the island for lunch, or simply coffee and cake. Victoria is originally from Devon and thus knows her way around a scone, with the result that the cream teas – sweet or savoury – are the best choice on the menu. If you're here on a sunny day, opt for the outdoor seating and enjoy the lovely views as you eat. £

Cafés

Final Checkout

MAP PAGE 106
Baltasound, ZE2 9TW. http://facebook.com/finalcheckout.
This convenience store in Baltasound has a handy little café, perfect for a breakfast roll or a jacket potato for lunch. Though not open in the evenings, if you're staying on Unst for a couple of days it's a godsend. £

Pub

Balta Light

MAP PAGE 106
Baltasound, ZE2 9TW. http://facebook.com/BaltaLightBar.
Britain's most northerly pub, the Balta Light is a barebones but friendly little place with a well-stocked bar. It sometimes does evening meals; check the Facebook page to see whether they're serving while you're on the island.

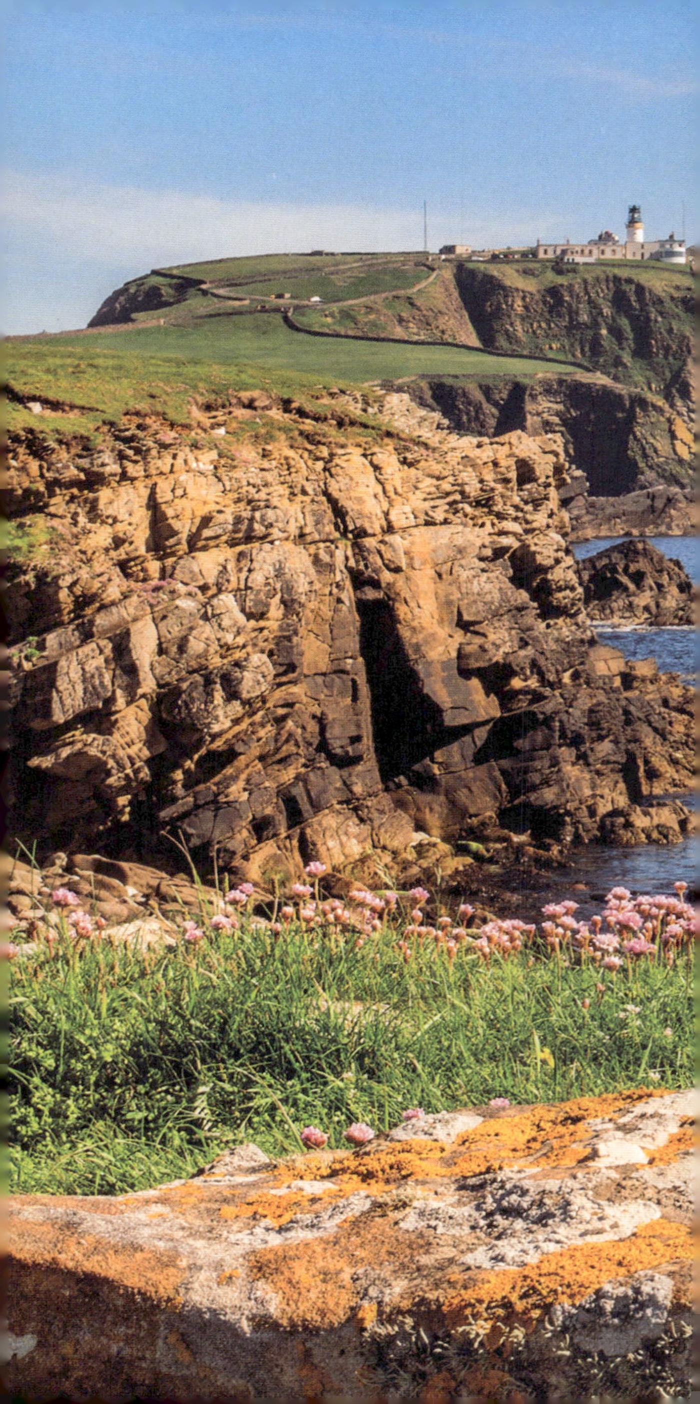

ACCOMMODATION

Sumburgh Lighthouse

Accommodation

There's a good range of accommodation on Shetland, with hotels, B&Bs, hostels, self-catering places and campsites all well-represented. There are plenty of options in the south and central Mainland, though it's worth bearing in mind that B&Bs in Lerwick tend to be better value than hotels. It'll take a little more effort to find places to stay on the islands, but by and large, there'll be something available – though be sure to book in advance, as rooms can be limited in peak season. Also remember that self-catering places (and the occasional B&B) tend to require minimum stays of at least three nights, though this may be negotiable in low season. If you have the equipment for it, wild camping or overnighting in your motorhome is always an option, though be aware that you must comply with the Scottish Outdoor Access Code (http://outdooraccess-scotland.scot).

Lerwick

EDDLEWOOD GUESTHOUSE MAP PAGE 26. 8 Clairmont Pl, Lerwick, ZE1 0BR. www.eddlewoodguesthouse.com. Occupying a grand old townhouse a few minutes' walk from Commercial Street, this comfortable guesthouse offers five bedrooms across three floors. There's a continental breakfast available in the mornings, and the owners are friendly. ££

THE GRAND HOTEL MAP PAGE 26. 149 Commercial St, Lerwick, ZE1 0AN. http://grandhotelshetland.co.uk. Located right in the centre of town, the Grand Hotel is a gloriously Gothic building dating back to the late nineteenth century. Although inside it's beginning to look a little tired, it's still an atmospheric place to stay, with friendly staff, comfy rooms and good breakfasts. ££

ISLESBURGH HOUSE HOSTEL MAP PAGE 26. King Harald St, Lerwick, ZE1 0EQ. http://shetland.gov.uk/islesburgh-community-centre-hostel/islesburgh-house-hostel. The best budget choice in Lerwick, Islesburgh House Hostel offers plenty of beds in mixed dorms, as well as multiple private rooms, some of which have their own bathrooms. It's a well-located place, just a short walk from Commercial Street, and has great facilities, including a kitchen, games room and secure bike storage. £

NORLANDE GUEST HOUSE MAP PAGE 26. 60 St Olaf St, Lerwick, ZE1 0EN. http://blyde-tae-bide.co.uk. One of Lerwick's best B&Bs, Norlande Guest House has four rooms, ranging from the luxurious St Ninian's – complete with a four-poster bed – to the cosy Peerie Snug, ideal for a single traveller. The friendly welcome, tasty continental breakfast and central but quiet location all combine to make this a very good choice. ££

Accommodation prices

One night's accommodation for two people, including breakfast:
£££ = over £110
££ = £75–110
£ = under £75

Up Helly Aa and Wool Week

Although there's usually no trouble booking accommodation on Shetland, places do tend to get very busy during popular events. In particular, if you're looking to visit for Up Helly Aa or Wool Week, you may want to consider booking a place to stay fairly early.

ROCKVILLA GUEST HOUSE MAP PAGE 26. 88 St Olaf St, Lerwick, ZE1 0ES. http://rockvillaguesthouse.com. A lovely B&B with three spacious bedrooms, all en-suite, in a well-located and quiet part of town. The full Scottish breakfast is top-notch, and the friendly owners can arrange tours around Shetland's Mainland. A separate self-catering apartment is also available. £££

Bressay and Noss

MARYFIELD HOUSE HOTEL MAP PAGE 36. Bressay, ZE2 9EL. http://maryfieldhousehotel.co.uk. The lovely Maryfield House Hotel offers three comfy rooms, with lovely views across the sound to Lerwick. The hotel's restaurant supplies mouth-watering evening meals, and there's a delightful bar to relax in too. It's ideally located, close to the ferry terminal. £££

South Mainland

BEN END B&B MAP PAGE 42. Fladdabister, ZE2 9HA. http://bnbholiday.com/Benendbandb. There's only one guest room at Ben End, so nab it if you can: it's a great place to stay, with a large and comfy bed ensuring a great night's sleep, and a top-notch lounge available for your exclusive use. If it's warm weather, there's also a lovely garden to relax and unwind in, and if you're very lucky you might befriend the beautiful resident cat, Hector. ££

HAYHOULL B&B MAP PAGE 42. Bigton, Hayhoull, ZE2 9JA. http://bedandbreakfastshetland.co.uk. A lovely B&B close to St Ninian's, with splendid views down over the tombolo, Hayhoull offers four bedrooms, two of which are en-suite and the other two with shared bathroom. There's a comfy lounge in which to relax after a day's exploring. Breakfasts are excellent, and delicious evening meals are available by prior arrangement. ££

SUMBURGH HOTEL MAP PAGE 42. Sumburgh, ZE3 9JN. http://sumburghhotel.com. The Sumburgh Hotel has an appropriately grand and Gothic exterior, given that it was built in the nineteenth century as a home for the local laird. Inside, the rooms are comfortable and well-kept, and the service is very friendly. Some areas could arguably do with a bit of modernising, but on the other hand, the time-warp feeling is quite agreeable. £££

SUMBURGH LIGHTHOUSE MAP PAGE 42. Sumburgh, ZE3 9JN. http://shetlandlighthouse.com. The self-catering accommodation in the lighthouse keeper's cottage at Sumburgh Head makes for a unique and hugely enjoyable stay. It's a lovely cosy place, with outstanding views, which has been sympathetically renovated and boasts all mod cons. Sleeps five. Minimum seven-night stay applies. £££

VOORTREKKER SHETLAND MAP PAGE 42. Southpunds, Levenwick ZE2 9HX. http://shetlandislandsaccommodation.co.uk. A trio of excellent self-catering apartments, all stylishly decorated and boasting gorgeous views out across the eastern coast of the Mainland. It's an ideal place to base yourself to explore the south, and there's even an on-site sauna for unwinding at the end of the day. Minimum stays apply. Adults only. £££

Fair Isle

AULD HAA GUESTHOUSE MAP PAGE 52. Fair Isle, ZE2 9JU. http://fair-isle.blogspot.com/p/b-b.html. This quirky but welcoming B&B is one of Fair Isle's few overnight options. There are two bedrooms, with shared bathroom. Evening meals are available, and it's well worth spending some time with the hugely knowledgeable owner, Tommy, while planning your exploration of this remote island. £££

Central Mainland

ERVHOUSE B&B MAP PAGE 58. A971, Huxter, Weisdale, ZE2 9LQ. http://shetlandcoastalcottages.co.uk/ervhouse. Without a doubt one of Shetland's finest B&Bs, Ervhouse occupies a splendid 1850s house on the shore of Weisdale Voe. Its rooms are welcoming and extremely comfortable, and there's a delightfully old-fashioned lounge with a warm log burner, where you can relax after a long day's exploring. Best of all, there are delicious evening meals available. Genuinely feels like a home away from home. £

GLEN B&B MAP PAGE 58. The Glen, Hamnavoe, West Burra, ZE2 9JY. http://glenbbshetland.co.uk. A welcoming B&B in the quiet village of Hamnavoe in the northwest corner of West Burra, Glen's five bedrooms are cosy and comfortable. Breakfast is delicious, and the friendly owner Elizabeth has put together an excellent information pack for visitors which can hugely help with your planning. ££

HERRISLEA HOUSE HOTEL MAP PAGE 58. Tingwall, Veensgarth, ZE2 9SB. http://herrisleahouse.co.uk. A friendly hotel occupying a grand old building, Herrislea offers nine bedrooms ranging from singles to a large family room. Dinner is available in the attractive dining room, and there's a lovely lounge – with a magnificent old ceiling – for relaxing in the evenings. ££

SCALLOWAY HOTEL MAP PAGE 60. Main St, Scalloway, ZE1 0TR. http://scallowayhotel.scot. A relatively large hotel on the seafront, the Scalloway Hotel offers comfortable and snug rooms, with a slightly old-fashioned feel. It's conveniently located and has a good restaurant and bar, but is arguably a tad overpriced. £££

Westside

BURNS COTTAGE MAP PAGE 72. Foula, ZE2 9PN. http://selfcateringfoula.co.uk. One of the best choices on Foula, Burns Cottage is a lovely self-catering spot in a renovated croft house. It sleeps up to six people and is centrally located, offering easy access to virtually anywhere on the island. £

BURRASTOW HOUSE MAP PAGE 66. Walls, ZE2 9PD. http://burrastowhouse.co.uk. A lovely small hotel in a remote location southwest of the settlement of Walls, Burrastow House is a great find. Housed in an eighteenth-century laird's house, the six rooms and the relaxing lounge are beautifully decorated, and there are delicious evening meals available. There's also a lovely self-catering cottage on the estate. £££

SKELD CARAVAN PARK AND CAMPSITE MAP PAGE 66. Skeld, ZE2 9NY. http://skeldcaravanpark.co.uk. A great spot for motorhomes and tents at the marina of the little village of Skeld, with well-maintained facilities including toilets, showers, a self-catering kitchen and a laundry room. £

Northeast Mainland

BRAE HOTEL MAP PAGE 76. Brae, ZE2 9QJ. http://braehotel.co.uk. The large Brae hotel has a fairly Scandi exterior, but inside it's a pretty corporate place, with perfectly clean and comfortable rooms without much in the way of character. Try to get a room at the side or back, as those at the front can get road noise. The restaurant is decent enough, while the attached bar is a very friendly and sometimes lively spot. £££

BUSTA HOUSE HOTEL MAP PAGE 76. Busta, ZE2 9QN. http://bustahouse.com. A marvellous hotel occupying a former laird's house, some parts of which date back to the late sixteenth century. The rooms are all beautifully decorated and spotless, each one themed after a different Shetland island, while downstairs there's an excellent restaurant and a fantastically decadent lounge to relax in. If you're feeling ambitious, you could try to work your way through the menu of 250 whiskies. £££

VOXTER OUTDOOR CENTRE MAP PAGE 76. Off A976, ZE2 9QP. http://voxteroutdoorcentre.co.uk. A former manse house now operating as accommodation, with twenty beds spread across three dormitories, as well as two private rooms with en-suite bathrooms. It's only useful if you're part of a large group, as the entire centre needs to be booked, with a minimum of ten guests. In peak season, stays must be three nights or more. ££

Whalsay and the Out Skerries

AULD MANSE MAP PAGE 80. Marrister, Whalsay, ZE2 9AE. http://facebook.com/AuldManseWhalsay. A beautifully kept B&B on Whalsay's west coast, with great views towards the Mainland, comfy bedrooms and excellent breakfasts. Evening meals are occasionally available – check when booking. ££

ROCKLEA RETREAT MAP PAGE 84. Bruray, Out Skerries, ZE2 9AR. http://rocklearetreat.co.uk. Possibly one of the remotest B&Bs you can find in the UK, Rocklea Retreat is also one of the friendliest. With two comfy rooms, a guest lounge, and kitchen facilities available should you wish to self-cater, the welcoming hosts Kia and Paul can also offer evening meals on request. Without a doubt the best place to stay on the Skerries. £££

Northmavine

BRAEWICK CARAVAN PARK MAP PAGE 88. Braewick, ZE2 9RS. 01806 202345. With plenty of space for motorhomes and tents, this is an ideal spot to base yourself for exploring the wilds of the north. You can hook up to water and electricity, and there are toilets, showers and laundry facilities. There are also some Wigwam camping cabins here, and it's on the same site as the excellent Braewick Café. £

ST MAGNUS BAY HOTEL MAP PAGE 88. Hillswick, ZE2 9RW. http://stmagnusbayhotel.co.uk. One of Shetland's most distinctive hotels, St Magnus Bay occupies a splendid Norwegian style wood timber building. Inside, the lobby and restaurant keep up the Norse theme, with wood panelling on the walls, as well as Viking shields and weapons. The bedrooms themselves have a slightly old-fashioned air, but they're spotless and very comfortable. £££

Yell

BURRAVOE CARAVAN SITE MAP PAGE 96. Burravoe, Yell, ZE2 9AY. http://shetland.org/listings/burravoe-pier-trust-caravan-and-campsite. Community-run caravan site based at Burravoe's marina, with space for eight motorhomes and four tent pitches. There are laundry facilities as well as toilets and showers. It's very good value, but bear in mind that advance booking is not possible. £

QUAM B&B MAP PAGE 96. West Sandwick, Yell, ZE2 9BH. http://spanglefish.com/Quam/index.asp. With a lovely location just above the West Sandwick beach, Quam B&B boasts splendid sea views. The bedrooms are cosy and comfortable, and the cooked-to-order breakfasts are truly excellent. It's just a short hop from here to the ferry to Mainland. £

Fetlar

FETLAR LODGE MAP PAGE 101. Houbie, Fetlar, ZE2 9DJ. http://fetlarlodge.com. This lovely self-catering place was once the home of the gardener for the grand Leagarth House, which is just next door. The Lodge sleeps six people across three bedrooms, and is ideally situated in Houbie, Fetlar's largest settlement. Also on site is the smaller Peerie House, which can sleep one or two people. ££

Unst

GARDIESFAULD HOSTEL MAP PAGE 106. Uyeasound, Unst, ZE2 9DW. http://independenthostels.co.uk/members/gardiesfauldhostel. The best budget accommodation option on Unst, Gardiesfauld offers camping and motorhome facilities plus 35 beds spread across five dormitories and private rooms. Kitchen facilities are excellent and there's a delightful conservatory in which to relax. £

MAILERSTA B&B MAP PAGE 106. Uyeasound, Unst, ZE2 9DL. 01957 755344. A warm welcome awaits at Mailersta B&B, which has two very comfortable guest rooms. It's a great base for exploring the southern part of Unst. Top-notch breakfasts are served in a lovely dining room with splendid views down to Uyeasound. ££

FIV

ESSENTIALS

Boarding the ferry to Yell, Unst and Fetlar

Arrival

Shetland's location in the middle of the North Sea means that its nearest cities are Aberdeen and Inverness; occupying third place is Bergen in Norway, which is considerably closer than other Scottish contenders. As such, getting here isn't particularly quick, and you may need to allow a couple of days for travel.

By air

The fastest way to reach Shetland is by plane. The only flights are operated by Loganair (http://loganair.co.uk), with routes to Sumburgh Airport from numerous cities including Aberdeen, Edinburgh, Glasgow and Inverness in Scotland, Kirkwall in Orkney, Bergen in Norway, and London Heathrow. The flights from London take 3 hours 30 minutes, but otherwise all flight times are less than 2 hours.

The main downside of flying is the cost: with only one operator, there's little incentive to keep prices down and fares can be eye-wateringly expensive. Also bear in mind that if you fly, you'll need to then hire a car on arrival – which is also pricey – or rely on public transport and accept that your ability to explore in depth will be a bit limited.

By ferry

There are a couple of ferry routes to Shetland in operation, of which the most commonly used is the Aberdeen to Lerwick passage. This takes between 12 and 14 hours, running overnight on a large ship with multiple facilities, including a restaurant, bar and even a cinema. Prices vary depending on the accommodation you choose: most expensive are the cabins with proper beds, but there are also 'sleeping pods' (a fancy name for what is essentially just a large reclining chair, though you are given a pillow and blanket), while the cheapest option is to simply sleep in the passenger lounge areas on regular chairs.

The other route runs from Kirkwall in Orkney to Lerwick, a journey of about 8 hours that's particularly ideal if you're looking to take in both of Scotland's northernmost archipelagos. This service is aboard the same ship as the one from Aberdeen; the ferry simply calls in at Kirkwall en route.

Both of these routes are operated by Northlink Ferries (http://northlinkferries.co.uk). They offer very good value if you're a foot passenger only, but the costs do mount up pretty quickly if you're bringing a vehicle and/or if you book a cabin or sleeping pod. Even so, the ferries are still usually considerably cheaper than the plane.

Reaching the ferry terminal

Aberdeen's ferry terminal is right in the city centre, conveniently located just a ten-minute walk from both the train and bus stations. If you're arriving by car, you'll most likely approach from the south along the A90, from which the terminal is signposted.

Getting around

The easiest way to explore Shetland is with your own car, but it's by no means impossible for those using public transport. Bus services cover Mainland fairly extensively, though you'll need to plan your time carefully to ensure you get the best out of them. To reach the islands, you'll find the regular ferries extremely handy, and there are also inter-island flights to Fair Isle and Foula.

Driving

Driving on Shetland is extremely easy, with wide and well-maintained A-roads running the length of Mainland, Yell and Unst north to south, providing access to most of the top sights. A network of good B-roads expands from the central route, and these tend to give way to smaller, often single-track roads as you head further from the main road. Even these are easy to navigate, with plenty of passing places and little other traffic.

Shetland is also well set up for exploring in motorhomes, with plenty of caravan sites dotted around the islands offering electrical hook-ups and overnight facilities. Although most roads are wide and perfectly suitable for motorhomes, extra care is needed when venturing down the smaller single-track roads. Make sure you'll have room to turn around before heading down a route that looks potentially narrow.

There are petrol garages found across the islands, with even surprisingly small settlements sometimes boasting pumps. Don't expect these to be 24-hour though; even in Lerwick, petrol stations close at 10pm.

Parking is generally easy and free: even in Lerwick, there are plenty of spots not far from the centre where you won't need to pay. A couple of major attractions (such as Jarlshof and the Muckle Roe Lighthouse walk, for example) have reasonably large dedicated parking areas, but otherwise it's just a matter of finding a convenient and considerate place to leave your car. In particular, make sure you haven't parked in a place marked as a turning area.

Vehicle hire is available on Shetland through local companies such as Bolt (http://boltscarhire.co.uk), who have been operating since the 1970s and can offer both cars and motorhomes. Another reliable operator is Jim's Garage (http://rental.jimsgarageford.co.uk). Both companies are based in Lerwick, but can arrange pick-up in other locations, such as Sumburgh Airport.

Buses

Shetland has a fairly extensive bus network, involving several different operators, which can get you between the major settlements and to some of the top tourist attractions. Routes extend across Mainland and around Yell and Unst. The most popular routes are pleasingly frequent, and you'll find it's perfectly possible to base yourself in Lerwick and do day trips out using the bus routes. Timetables can be viewed at http://zettrans.org.uk/travel/public-transport/bus, while you can check live departures at http://travel.shetland.org/desktop_bus_timetables.php.

Note that some of the less frequently used bus routes only operate on demand, with the Dial a Ride service. If you want to use these, you'll need to call 01595 745745 a day in advance to book it. Dial a Ride routes are marked on the timetable as DAR. Using Dial a Ride, you'll be able to access some fairly remote spots such as Esha Ness, without recourse to taking a taxi.

Bus routes

Some of the most useful bus routes include the 4, linking Lerwick and Scalloway; the 6, which runs from Lerwick to Sumburgh via Jarlshof; the 9, from Lerwick to Walls on Westside; the 21, from Lerwick to Hillswick via Tingwall and Brae; the 23, from Lerwick to Toft (for the Yell ferry); the 24Y, running between Ulsta and Cullivoe on Yell, via Gutcher; and the 28, which covers Unst from Belmont to Baltasound.

Cycling

Shetland is an excellent destination for a cycling trip, thanks to its well-maintained and quiet roads and gorgeous scenery. Although it's not flat, it's for the most part relatively easy going, with only very rare times when you'll encounter a serious hill. Perhaps the holy grail for cyclists will be Skaw on Unst, which marks the northernmost point of the UK's National Cycle Route 1, a 2000-kilometre route with its southern terminus in Dover.

Bikes can be brought across on the Northlink Ferries, and it's also possible for them to be carried on Loganair flights. If you prefer to pick up bikes once on Shetland, there are rental shops in Lerwick, including the Shetland Community Bike Project (01595 690077) and Grantfield Garage (http://grantfieldgarage.co.uk/cycle-hire).

Walking

One of the principal attractions of a trip to Shetland is the wealth of marvellous walking country the islands offer. The vast majority of the best walks are coastal, with Westside and Northmavine in particular boasting some splendid routes: along the cliffs of Esha Ness, for example, or from Deepdale to Sandness. For a fairly challenging hike, consider the ascent of Ronas Hill, Shetland's highest point, with an optional extension to Langayre on Northmavine's west coast, one of the remotest places on the Mainland. There are plenty of great options for more casual walkers too, which include the Ness of Burgi near Sumburgh, or exploring Sandwick on Unst, among many more.

Ferries

You can access a good deal of Shetland without recourse to crossing the water, but if you want to explore the islands you'll need to use the ferries. Operated by Shetland Islands Council, there are frequent sailings to all the outlying islands, from numerous ports around Mainland. For Bressay, you'll depart from Lerwick; Whalsay and the Out Skerries from Vidlin or Laxo; Foula from Walls; Fair Isle from Grutness, near Sumburgh; Papa Stour from West Burrafirth; and Yell from Toft. For Unst and Fetlar, you'll need to first cross to Yell and then take the ferry from Gutcher.

You can check timetables and make bookings at http://shetland.gov.uk/ferries. Pre-booking is generally advisable – though in low season you can usually get away without – especially if you're heading to Unst: the ferry to Yell is pretty large, but the one to Unst is smaller, and it's not uncommon to find yourself waiting at Gutcher for an hour if you haven't pre-booked passage. Remember that it takes around half an hour to drive across Yell, so allow yourself enough time between ferries to make the journey; by and large, the timetables are designed to make sure travellers can get between the two terminals in time.

Air

Inter-island flights are only available to Fair Isle and Foula, both operating from Tingwall Airport. These routes are operated by Airtask Group. Timetables can be found at http://airtask.com/passenger-transport, while bookings must be made by phone (01595 840246) or email (lwk.ops@airtask.com).

Directory A-Z

Accessible travel

Shetland is dedicated to making visits as accessible as possible, with a variety of online resources which are worth a look before travelling. For accommodation, you can search https://stay.shetland.org and use the accessibility filter, and if you're looking for a tour, consider browsing http://shetland.org/visit/do/trips to locate operators who offer wheelchair-friendly trips. Local charity Ability Shetland (http://abilityshetland.com), based in Lerwick, is a fantastic organisation which offers all-terrain wheelchairs and specially adapted cycles available to borrow for free. The local buses are also wheelchair-friendly, as are several attractions such as the Shetland Museum in Lerwick.

Addresses

Outside Lerwick and other larger settlements such as Scalloway and Brae, most addresses consist simply of a village name and postcode, with road names a relative rarity, and house numbers largely unknown. Mapping apps are generally very reliable and will get you where you need to be.

Children

Although there are few attractions aimed specifically at children on Shetland, it's still a great destination for little ones. The lovely beaches are likely to prove very popular, despite the cold water: some of the very best sandy choices include the Sands of Meal on West Burra, Breckon Sands on Yell, and Skaw Beach on Unst. Children are also likely to be enthralled by the considerable oddness of the tombolo at St Ninian's Isle.

Kids with an interest in history may enjoy sites such as Jarlshof and the Broch of Mousa, and will probably love the sight of the Viking longboat at Haroldswick on Unst. Those keen on wildlife, meanwhile, will be delighted by the opportunity to spot whales, dolphins and puffins at places such as Sumburgh Head and Noss. Other kid-friendly wildlife attractions include the Shetland Pony Experience and the Outpost. Museums-wise, there are few in Shetland that are likely to be particularly engaging for children, though the Shetland Museum in Lerwick does at least make an effort. You could also consider a trip to Michaelswood on Westside, a woodland area containing large models of dinosaurs.

Children are almost always welcome at pubs and restaurants, as well as at most accommodation, though occasionally B&Bs will not accept anyone under twelve years old, so you'd be advised to check at the time of booking. Self-catering options are perhaps the best choice when holidaying with children, though camping is also likely to be a memorable adventure.

Cinema

Shetland's cinema, the Mareel (http://shetlandarts.org/venues/mareel), is found at Lerwick's harbour in a striking building which also acts as a community hub. It shows current major releases, as well as the occasional older film and simulcast of theatre performances.

Crime and emergencies

Despite apparent evidence to the contrary in the TV series *Shetland*, Shetland isn't a hotbed of crime. You are unlikely to have any need for the emergency services, but if you need them, you can contact the police, fire brigade, ambulance or coastguard on 999, or in non-emergency cases 101.

Discount passes

Many of Shetland's historic sites are operated by Historic Environment Scotland (http://historicenvironment.scot). Entry to the vast majority of them is free, but where charges apply (notably at Jarlshof), Historic Environment Scotland members enter for free. English Heritage (http://english-heritage.org.uk) and Cadw (http://cadw.gov.wales) members are entitled to half-price entry if it's within one year of joining, or free entry if longer.

> ### Eating prices
> Two course meal for one person, including a drink:
> ££££ = over £40
> £££ = £25 to £40
> ££ = £10–25
> £ = under £10

Electricity
Shetland uses standard UK plug sockets. The current is 240V AC. North American appliances will need a transformer and adaptor; those from Europe, South Africa, Australia and New Zealand only need an adaptor.

Health
Shetland's hospital is the Gilbert Bain Hospital (South Rd, Lerwick, ZE1 0TB, http://nhsshetland.scot/gilbert-bain-hospital), which has an A&E service, as well as plenty of non-emergency care. Since 2021, there have been plans to construct a new hospital to replace Gilbert Bain, but these have not progressed far at time of writing.

There are ten GP surgeries across Shetland, including several on Mainland, with others on the larger islands. A full list, including opening hours, can be found at http://nhsshetland.scot/general-practice. Dental surgeries can be found in Lerwick and Brae, and on Yell and Whalsay: a full list is available at http://nhsshetland.scot/dental/dental-practices. Pharmacies are found only on Shetland's Mainland, although it's often possible to obtain minor medications such as paracetamol from general stores on the islands.

Internet
Mobile coverage is generally good across most of Shetland, and it's a rare occasion when you'll find yourself out of signal. Even so, if you're relying on something – a mapping app, for example – it could be advisable to download an offline version before setting off on a lengthy hike in a remote area.

Left luggage
There's a left luggage service at the ferry terminal in Lerwick, or your accommodation will usually be happy to hold onto your bags for the day after you've checked out, if needed.

LGBTQ+
Shetland is LGBTQ+ friendly, but there isn't a particularly vibrant scene. Shetland Pride (http://shetlandpride.co.uk) put on an annual Pride festival, as well as several other events throughout the year.

Lost property
Shetland's police have an interactive online form (http://scotland.police.uk/secureforms/lost-property) to complete if you have lost something. There are also two Lost and Found groups (http://tinyurl.com/pfkn2bh5 or http://tinyurl.com/5askz67h) on Facebook, which can be quite handy for reuniting owners with missing items.

Money
The UK's currency is the pound sterling (£), divided into 100 pence (p). Coins come in denominations of 1p, 2p, 5p, 10p, 20p, 50p, £1 and £2. Most of Shetland's cash machines will dispense Scottish banknotes, which come in denominations of £1, £5, £10, £20, £50 and £100, though the £1 note is now rarely seen. The £100 note is also not particularly common. £100 and £50 notes are sometimes met with suspicion by traders.

Generally speaking, contactless or chip and pin card payments are accepted everywhere, though in some cases – particularly in B&Bs – you're still going to need cash. ATMs and banks can be found easily in Lerwick and in larger settlements such as Scalloway and Brae, as well as on some of the islands, but it's wise to take cash with you when leaving the Mainland.

Opening hours

Opening hours in Shetland can be limited and vary between seasons. Shops tend to keep relatively standard business hours, and can generally be relied upon to be open Monday to Saturday between 10am and 4pm at the least. Cafés and restaurants usually serve food between around noon and 3pm, then again from 6pm to 9pm, though – particularly in Lerwick – some might be open throughout the day. Attractions, particularly the local museums on the islands, often have less standard opening times, sometimes being limited to a couple of days per week. Several attractions close entirely over the winter, though most operate round the year with reduced hours in winter. It's therefore best to double-check before travelling if you are intending to visit a particular place.

Post offices

Post offices are found in all the main settlements on Mainland and on most of the islands, with most branches open Monday to Friday between 9am and 5pm. Specific branch opening hours can be checked online at www.postoffice.co.uk/branch-finder.

Public holidays

Public holidays (Bank Holidays) observed in Shetland are:
January 1
January 2
Good Friday
First Monday in May
Last Monday in May
First Monday in August
November 30
December 25
December 26

Note that if January 1, January 2, November 30, December 25 or December 26 fall on a Saturday or Sunday, the next weekday becomes a public holiday.

Smoking

Smoking is illegal in all indoor public spaces in Shetland, including public transport, museums, pubs and restaurants. It is also illegal to smoke in a private vehicle if there is a person under the age of 18 in the vehicle. Vaping (e-cigarettes) is not covered by either of these laws, but it is banned on public transport, and individual establishments have the right to prohibit it on their premises: if unsure, check with the proprietor. Note that the sale of single-use vapes will be banned in Shetland from June 2025.

Time

Greenwich Mean Time (GMT) – equivalent to Coordinated Universal Time (UTC) – is used from the end of October to the end of March; for the rest of the year Britain switches to British Summer Time (BST), one hour ahead of GMT. GMT is five hours ahead of the US Eastern Standard Time and ten hours behind Australian Eastern Standard Time.

Tipping

There are no specific rules, but waiting staff in restaurants will usually expect a ten to fifteen percent tip. This tends to apply less in pubs and cafés where you pay for your food in advance, though in these places you may find a jar by the till for tips. Note that some restaurants, usually in the more upmarket places, will add a discretionary service charge – you are not obliged to pay this, particularly if you felt the food or service wasn't up to scratch.

Toilets

Public toilets are relatively common across Shetland: they're found at many car parks, in towns and villages, and at ferry terminal waiting rooms. There's no charge for using them.

Tourist information

Until November 2024, Shetland's Tourist Centre, in central Lerwick (Market Cross, ZE1 0LU), was an incredibly helpful office, offering advice on practicalities such as ferry timetables, as well as help with planning itineraries and suggesting places to visit. It was closed by VisitScotland as part of a drive to move services online, but will hopefully resurface as a local initiative. In the meantime, you can often find information at local museums and heritage centres, as they're usually staffed by extremely knowledgeable people. Handy online information can be found at http://shetland.org/visit and http://visitscotland.com/places-to-go/islands/Shetland.

Festivals and events

Up Helly Aa

January http://uphellyaa.org
Up Helly Aa is the biggest event on Shetland's calendar. Held in the depths of winter, this fire festival sees hundreds of costumed squads march through the streets of Lerwick, bearing torches which are subsequently used to burn a replica Viking longship. There's then a fireworks display, followed by the squads performing comic skits at several venues around the town. Most other settlements around Shetland have their own versions of the Up Helly Aa, but Lerwick's is the largest and most spectacular. If you're planning on attending, make sure to book accommodation early.

Shetland Folk Festival

May http://shetlandfolkfestival.com
One of Shetland's top musical events, the Folk Festival attracts plenty of local talent as well as national and international performers. Concerts are held in various venues across Shetland, including at Mareel in Lerwick.

Shetland Classic Motor Show

June
http://shetlandclassicmotorshow.co.uk
Classic car enthusiasts make their way to Lerwick for this biennial show, which features displays of more than 300 vehicles – both cars and motorbikes – at the Clickimin Leisure Centre. Many of the vehicles are taken on drives around Shetland, so even if you're not attending the show, keep your eyes out for them if you happen to be in Shetland at the time.

Shetland Pride

June http://shetlandpride.co.uk
Shetland's principal LGBTQ+ event, involving live music, drag shows and a fantastic costumed parade through Lerwick.

Shetland Race

June http://shetlandrace.no
An annual yachting race from Bergen in Norway to Lerwick; even if you're not participating, it's enjoyable to be in Lerwick in time to see the competing yachts sail into the harbour.

Simmer Dim Rally

June http://tinyurl.com/2zhyhj83
Timed to coincide with the summer solstice, the Simmer Dim Rally sees motorbike enthusiasts make their way to the UK's northernmost bike rally. There's a programme of live music and fun games. The Rally has been going since 1982, and there's a loyal cohort who still attend every year.

Unst Fest

July http://facebook.com/UnstFest
A week of events based on the northern island of Unst, which among much else includes live music, fun competitions, food and drink, and costumed parades.

Shetland Fiddle Week

August http://shetlandfiddleweek.com
Shetland's traditional fiddle music is celebrated during this small event, which offers fiddle classes for everyone from beginners to experts. If you prefer to listen rather than play, there are also evening fiddle concerts held at various locations throughout the week.

Wool Week

September/October
http://shetlandwoolweek.com
One of Shetland's most popular festivals, Wool Week sees knitting enthusiasts from across the world arrive on the islands for an extensive programme of workshops, events and tours. Wool Week's events are held all over Shetland, and are charged separately, so you can put together your own programme depending on your personal interests. Accommodation can get pretty busy for Wool Week, so consider booking early.

Shetland Accordion and Fiddle Festival

October
http://shetlandaccordionandfiddle.com
A celebration of traditional Scottish music and dancing, with events held in numerous locations across Shetland but centring on Lerwick. The main event of the festival is the Grand Dance, with multiple local bands providing music for a six-hour dance spectacle.

Chronology

c.4400 BC Arrival of first humans in Shetland.

c.2000 BC First settlement at Jarlshof.

c.100 BC Mousa Broch constructed.

c.700 Christianity arrives in Shetland.

9th century Shetland colonised by the Norse.

c.875 Opponents of the Norwegian king Harald Fairhair base themselves in Shetland, forcing Harald to lead an expedition to subdue them. Harald makes his ally Rognvald the first Earl of Orkney and Shetland.

995 Along with the rest of Norway, Shetland officially adopts Christianity as the state religion.

1195 The King of Norway takes direct control of Shetland, taking over from the Earls of Orkney.

1260s Scotland goes to war with Norway for control of Norwegian-owned Northern Isles. Norway loses the Isle of Man and the Hebrides, but retains Orkney and Shetland.

1349 Shetland suffers under the Black Death.

14th century The Hanseatic League becomes Shetland's main trading partner, ushering in an era of relative prosperity that lasts several hundred years.

1469 Shetland (along with Orkney) becomes part of Scotland, as a dowry for the marriage of Princess Margrethe of Denmark and James III of Scotland.

1588 *El Gran Grifón*, one of the Spanish Armada's flagships, is shipwrecked off Fair Isle.

1593 Patrick Stewart becomes Earl of Orkney, quickly becoming notorious for his tyrannical rule over Orkney and Shetland.

1600 Construction of Scalloway Castle begins.

1667 Negotiations for the Treaty of Breda, at the end of the Second Anglo-Dutch War, is the last time Norway attempts to recover Shetland.

1707 The Act of Union, merging the Kingdoms of England and Scotland, bans Shetland's trade with the Hanseatic League, resulting in economic downturn.

1708 Lerwick becomes capital of Shetland, displacing Scalloway.

1820s The worst clearances in Shetland take place in Fetlar, as local landowner Sir Arthur Nicolson evicts crofters from their homes.

c.1850 Death of Walter Sutherland, the last documented speaker of Shetland's Norn language.

1860s to 1880s Facing difficult economic conditions at home, at least 8000 Shetlanders emigrate, heading for destinations as far afield as Canada and New Zealand.

1881 The first Up Helly Aa torch procession is held, with the event developing in scope over the course of the next 20 years.

1881 58 fishermen die in a storm off Gloup, on the island of Yell. The disaster may have contributed to the decline of the haaf fishing system.

1936 Sumburgh Airport opens, with its first flight arriving from Aberdeen on 3 June.

1937 The film *The Edge of the World*, depicting the depopulation of the island of St Kilda, is filmed on Foula.

1940 The Shetland Bus operations begin during World War II, initially based out of Lunna and subsequently moving to Scalloway.

1978 Sullom Voe Oil Terminal opens, boosting Shetland's economy and leading to development of the islands' infrastructure.

1996 Bobby's Bus Shelter on Unst is decorated and furnished for the first time.

2010 The Wool Week festival is held for the first time.

2012 A message in a bottle launched in 1914 is found off Fetlar. At the time of its discovery, it was the oldest known message in a bottle to be recovered.

2013 The popular BBC crime drama series *Shetland* airs its first episode.

2020 Shetland enters lockdown for the COVID-19 pandemic, at one point having the highest number of cases in Scotland relative to its population.

2022 Construction of the SaxaVord Spaceport begins on Unst.

2023 Up Helly Aa squads allow women to participate for the first time.

2024 *Billy and Molly: An Otter Love Story* – an award-winning film telling the story of the friendship between a Shetland man and an otter – is released.

Language

Between the tenth and seventeenth centuries, the chief language of Shetland was Norn, a Scandinavian tongue close to modern Faroese and Icelandic. After the end of Norse rule, the Norn language gradually petered out, being replaced by Scots and English, and was virtually extinct by the eighteenth century. The last documented Norn speaker was Walter Sutherland, who lived at Skaw on the northern tip of Unst, and died around 1850, but it's possible that the language survived even longer on Foula.

Today, Shetland has its own dialect, and individual islands and communities have local variations. The dialects have a Scots base, with some Old Norse words, but they don't sound strongly Scottish. Listed below are some of the words you're most likely to hear, including some birds' names and common elements in place names.

Norn phrases and vocabulary

aak guillemot
alan storm petrel
ayre beach
bister farm
böd fisherman's store
bonxie great skua
bruck rubbish
burra heath rush
crö sheepfold
eela rod-fishing from small boats
fourareen four-oared boat
geo coastal inlet
gloup blowhole, behind a cliff face, where spray is blasted out from the cave below (from Old Norse *glup*, a throat)
haa laird's house
haaf deep-sea fishing. Lit. 'heave'
hap hand-knitted shawl
howe mound
kame ridge of hills
kishie basket
maa seagull
mool headland
muckle large
noost hollow place where a boat is drawn up
norie (or tammie-norie) puffin
noup steep headland
peerie small
plantiecrub (or plantiecrö) small dry-stone enclosure for growing cabbages
quoy enclosed, cultivated common land
roost tide race
scattald common grazing land
scord gap or pass in a ridge of hills
setter farm
simmer dim summer twilight
sixareen six-oared boat
solan gannet
soothmoother incomer
voe sea inlet
yoal rowing boat used for fishing

Publishing Information
First edition 2025

Distribution
UK, Ireland and Europe
Apa Publications (UK) Ltd; mail@roughguides.com
United States and Canada
Two Rivers; ips@ingramcontent.com
Australia and New Zealand
Woodslane; info@woodslane.com.au
Worldwide
Apa Publications (UK) Ltd; mail@roughguides.com

Special Sales, Content Licensing and CoPublishing
Rough Guides can be purchased in bulk quantities at discounted prices. We can create special editions, personalized jackets and corporate imprints tailored to your needs. mail@roughguides.com.
roughguides.com

EU Representative
LOGOS EUROPE, 9 rue Nicolas Poussin, 17000, LA ROCHELLE, France; Contact@logoseurope.eu; +33 (0) 667937378

Printed by Finidr in Czech Republic

ISBN: 9781835292273

This book was produced using **Typefi** automated publishing software.

A catalogue record for this book is available from the British Library.

All rights reserved
© 2025 Apa Digital AG
License edition © Apa Publications Ltd UK
Contains Ordnance Survey data © Crown copyright and database rights 2025

No part of this book may be reproduced, stored in a retrieval system, or transmitted in any form or by any means – electronic, mechanical, photocopying, recording, or otherwise – without prior written permission from Apa Publications.

The publishers and authors have done their best to ensure the accuracy and currency of all the information in **Pocket Rough Guide Shetland**, however, they can accept no responsibility for any loss, injury, or inconvenience sustained by any traveller as a result of information or advice contained in the guide.

Rough Guide Credits
Editor: Rachel Lawrence
Cartography: Carte
Picture manager: Tom Smyth
Layout: Ankur Guha
Original design: Richard Czapnik

Publishing technology manager: Rebeka Davies
Production operations manager: Katie Bennett
Head of Publishing: Sarah Clark

About the author
Owen Morton is based in North Yorkshire, and has written or contributed to numerous Rough Guides, ranging from Pembrokeshire to the Philippines. When not exploring the world, he entertains himself by writing a blog about 1980s cartoons. His favourite animal is the wonderfully expressive and permanently furious manul, native to Central Asia and sadly not Shetland. Follow him on Instagram at @owenmortonmanul.

Acknowledgements
Author: Thank you to the fantastic team at Rough Guides, particularly Rachel Lawrence. Many thanks to everybody who gave me so many hints and tips for exploring Shetland, including Gail Herculeson (in particular for putting me onto Culswick Broch and Deepdale), Jane Macauley (for the lovely afternoon on Unst), Jim Leask (for the great info on Yell and Unst), James Millington (for recommending walking spots on Northmavine, and for taking such inspiring photos), and Kariss Goodlad and Kieren Clubb (for the restaurant recommendations, and for a very pleasant evening at the Busta House Hotel). Thanks also to Lizzie and Andy Thomson for all their hints, especially St Ninian's Isle, and of course to Anderson Thomson for letting me play with his train set (nothing to do with Shetland, admittedly, but I'm still grateful). Thank you too to the staff at Whalsay Heritage Centre for the coffee and the fascinating chat, and at Bressay and Fetlar heritage centres for opening for me out of season. Thanks also go out to Anna Clarke for putting me onto Maps.Me, without which I'd have been lost on Shetland, both figuratively and literally. Finally, many thanks to Katherine Morton for her unending support.

Help us update
We've gone to a lot of effort to ensure that this edition of the **Pocket Rough Guide Shetland** is accurate and up-to-date. However, things change – places get "discovered", restaurants and rooms raise prices or lower standards, and businesses cease trading. If you feel we've got it wrong or left something out, we'd like to know, and if you can direct us to the web address, so much the better.

Please send your comments with the subject line "**Pocket Rough Guide Shetland Update**" to mail@roughguides.com. We'll send a copy of the next edition (or any other Rough Guide if you prefer) for the very best emails.

Photo Credits
(Key: T-top; C-centre; B-bottom; L-left; R-right)
Alamy 10, 13C, 14T, 16B, 17T, 51, 53, 93, 113
Owen Morten 20C, 37, 50, 70, 95, 99
Rachel Lawrence 59, 61
Shutterstock 1, 2T, 2BL, 2CR, 2BR, 4, 11T, 11B, 12/13T, 12B, 16T, 17B, 19T, 19B, 20T, 20B, 21T, 21C, 21B, 22/23, 25, 27, 29, 30, 31, 32, 34, 39, 40, 43, 44, 45, 47, 48, 54, 56, 62, 63, 64, 71, 73, 74, 81, 83, 90, 92, 107, 108, 112, 114/115

Vicky Brock 38
VisitScotland/Kenny Lam 12/13B, 14B, 15B, 18T, 24
VisitScotland/Paul Tomkins 15T, 18C, 18B, 19C, 79, 82, 86, 101, 103, 105, 110, 120/121

Cover: Shetland Pony on the Shetland Isles **Andrew J. Shearer/iStock**

Index

A

accessible travel 124
accommodation 116
  Auld Haa Guesthouse 118
  Auld Manse 119
  Ben End B&B 117
  Brae Hotel 119
  Braewick Caravan Park 119
  Burns Cottage 118
  Burrastow House 118
  Burravoe Caravan Site 119
  Busta House Hotel 119
  Eddlewood Guesthouse 116
  Ervhouse B&B 118
  Glen B&B 118
  Hayhoull B&B 117
  Herrislea House Hotel 118
  Islesburgh House Hostel 116
  Mayfield House Hotel 117
  Norlande Guest House 116
  Rocklea Retreat 119
  Rockvilla Guest House 117
  Scalloway Hotel 118
  Skeld Caravan Park and Campsite 118
  St Magnus Bay Hotel 119
  Sumburgh Hotel 117
  Sumburgh Lighthouse 117
  The Grand Hotel 116
  Voortrekker Shetland 117
  Voxter Outdoor Centre 119
addresses 125
Aith 102
Aith Ness 37
Aith Voe Harbour 41
arrival 122
  by air 122
  by ferry 122
Asta Golf Club 57

B

Baliasta Kirk 109
Baltasound 108
Bannaminn Beach 62
B&Bs 116
Belmont Longhouse 104
Beorgs of Housetter 91
Bixter 64
Bobby's Bus Shelter 109
Bonhoga Gallery 74
Breckon Sands 98
Bressay and Noss 34
Bressay Heritage Centre 34
Bressay Lighthouse 35
Broch of Burraland 45
Broch of Burraness 97
Broch of Clickimin 29
Brochs 44
Brough Kirk 83
Brough Lodge 100
Bruray 84
Burn of Lunklet 68
Burn of Valayre 78

C

Cabin Museum 75
cafés
  Braewick Café 93
  Fetlar Café 103
  Final Checkout 113
  Fjarà 33
  Frankie's Fish and Chips 79
  Hoswick Visitor Centre 51
  Isle Eat 99
  Speldiburn Café 39
  Sumburgh Head Observatory 51
  The Cornerstone 63
  The Dowry 33
  The Old Haa Tearoom 99
  The Original Cake Fridge 73
  Victoria's Vintage Tea Rooms 113
cafés (by area)
  Bressay and Noss 39
  Fetlar 103
  Lerwick and around 33
  Mainland, central 63
  Mainland, northeast 79
  Mainland, south 51
  Northmavine 93
  Unst 113
  Westside 73
  Yell 99
campsites 116
Carol's Ponies 57
Catalina Memorial 94
Catpund 43
children 125
chronology 129
cinema 125
Clivocast Standing Stone 104
Commercial Street 28
crime and emergencies 125
Cruester Burnt Mound 34
Cullingsbrough 37
Cullivoe 98
Culswick Broch 71
Cunningsburgh 43

D

Da Gairdins 73
Da Herra 97
Deepdale 70
Directory A-Z 124
discount passes 125
drinking 7

E

Earl Patrick Stewart 57
Easthouse Museum 62
eating 7
electricity 126
El Gran Grifón 55
Esha Ness 90

F

Fair Isle 52
Fair Isle knitwear 54
Fair Isle Observatory 52
Festivals and events 128
  Shetland Accordion and Fiddle Festival 129
  Shetland Classic Motor Show 128
  Shetland Fiddle Week 129
  Shetland Folk Festival 128
  Shetland Pride 128
  Shetland Race 128
  Simmer Dim Rally 129
  Unst Fest 129
  Up Helly Aa 128
  Wool Week 129
Fethaland 92
Fetlar 100
Fetlar Interpretative Centre 102
Fisherman's Memorial 35
Fladdabister 40, 41
Fort Charlotte 27
Foula 69
Fugla Ness 61
Funzie and the Snap 103

G

Garth's Croft 35
George Waterston Museum 55
getting around 122
  air 124
  buses 123
  by driving 123
  cycling 123
  ferries 124
  walking 124
getting to
  Bressay and Noss 35
  Fair Isle 53
  Fetlar 100
  Foula 69
  Out Skerries 82

Papa Stour 65
Unst 104
Whalsay 80
Yell 94
Giant's Leg 38
Girlsta Loch 74
Girlsta to Laxo 74
Gloup Fishermen's Memorial 99
Gossabrough 95
Gruting 103
Gruting folly walk 102
Grutwick 38
Gulberwick 40
Gunnersby Churchyard 37
Gunnister Man's Stone 86
Gutcher 98

H

Haaf fishing 98
Hagdale Horse Mill 110
Halligarth 108
Haltadans Stone Circle 100
Haroldswick 110, 111
Hay's Dock 24
health 126
Heogan 36
Hermanness Nature Reserve 111
Hillswick 87
Hillswick Seal Sanctuary 87
hostels 116
Hoswick Beach 46
Hoswick Visitor Centre 46
hotels 116
Houbie 101
Housay 85
Houss Ness 62
Huxter 70

I

internet 126
itineraries 18

J

Jarlshof 49

K

Kergord 74
King George V Park 28

L

Landberg 53
language 131
 Norn phrases 131
Laurence Bruce 107
Law Ting Holm 56
Leebitton Mousa Museum 43

left luggage 126
Lerwick 24
Lerwick Brewery 31
Lerwick Town Hall 27
Levenwick Beach 46
LGBTQ+ 126
Loch of Brough 37
Loch of Funzie 102
Loch of Huxter 82
Longhouses 105
lost property 126
Lund Standing Stone 107
Lunna 75
Lunna Ness 78
Lunnasting Stone 75

M

Mail 35
Mainland, central 56
Mainland, northeast 74
Main Street, Scalloway 60
Malcolm's Head 55
maps 6
 Bressay and Noss 36
 Fair Isle 52
 Fetlar 101
 Foula 72
 Lerwick and around 28
 Lerwick, centre 26
 Mainland, central 58
 Mainland, northeast 76
 Mainland, south 42
 Northmavine 88
 Out Skerries 84
 Papa Stour 68
 Scalloway 60
 Shetland at a glance 8
 Unst 106
 Westside 66
 Whalsay 80
 Yell 96
Mareel 25
Market Cross 29
Mavis Grind 86
Meal Beach 61
Michaelswood 64
Mid Yell 97
money 126
Mousa 43
Muness Castle 105

N

Ness of Burgi 48
Ness of Sound 30, 97
New Street, Scalloway 59
Noness 45
North Haven 52
North Lighthouse 54
Northmavine 86
Nort Trow Garden 91

Norwick Beach 112
Noss 39
Noss Sound 38

O

Old Scatness Broch and Iron Age Village 48
Ollaberry 90
opening hours 127
Out Skerries 84

P

Papa Stour 65
Pettigarth Field 82
Pier House Museum 80
Port Arthur 61
post offices 127
Potoz Plane 91
public holidays 127
pubs and bars
 Balta Light 113
 Da Noost 33
 The Douglas Inn 33
 The Kiln Bar 63
 Mid Brae Inn 79
 Northern Lights 79
 Welcome Inn 79
pubs and bars (by area)
 Lerwick and around 33
 Mainland, central 63
 Mainland, northeast 79
 Unst 113

Q

Quendale Mill 47

R

Reawick Beach 72
Rerwick Beach 46
Rescues and Wrecks Trail 36
restaurants
 Busta House Hotel 79
 C'est La Vie 32
 Da Haaf 63
 Da Steak Hoose 33
 LJ's Diner 99
 No 88 33
 Phu Siam 33
 Raba 33
 Scalloway Hotel 63
 St Magnus Bay Hotel 93
 Sumburgh Hotel 51
restaurants (by area)
 Fair Isle 55
 Lerwick and around 32
 Mainland, central 63
 Mainland, northeast 79
 Mainland, south 51

INDEX

Northmavine 93
Out Skerries 85
Whalsay 85
Yell 99
Ronas Hill 91

S

Sand Beach 73
Sandness 69
Sandwick 107
Sandwick Beach 45
Saxa Vord 111
Saxa Vord Distillery 111
SaxaVord Spaceport 112
Scalloway 57
Scalloway Castle 57
Scalloway Museum 59
Scord of Brouster 69
self-catering 116
Sheep Rock 54
Shetland Bus 59
Shetland Crofthouse Museum 47
Shetland Geopark 91
Shetland Library 28
Shetland Museum and Archives 24
Shetland Pony Experience 62
Shetland's böds 30
Shetland Textile Museum 31
shops 7
  Artery 63
  Burra Bears 63
  Da Peerie Rock Shop 113
  Esme Wilcock Jewellery 93
  Glansin Glass 113
  Hatchery Bookshop 79
  Island Larder 32
  Jamieson's of Shetland 32
  Julie Williamson Designs 85
  Karlin Anderson 51
  Lerwick Distillery Shop 32
  Nielanell 51
  Silly Sheep Fibre Company 73
  The Puffin Republic 32
  The Shetland Gallery 99
  The Shetland Times Bookshop 32

  Victoria's Vintage Tea Rooms 113
shops (by area)
  Lerwick and around 32
  Mainland, central 63
  Mainland, northeast 79
  Mainland, south 51
  Northmavine 93
  Unst 113
  Westside 73
  Whalsay 85
  Yell 99
Skaw Beach 112
smoking 127
Mainland 40
South Lighthouse 55
Spiggie Loch 47
Stanydale Temple 71
St Colman's Church 94
Stenness 87
St Laurence Kirk 61
St Magnus Church 94
St Ninian 46
St Ninian's Isle 46
St Olaf's Kirk 107
Sullom Voe 78
Sumburgh Head 50
Swedish Church Memorial 109
Symbister 80

T

Tangwick Haa Museum 87
The Edmondstons 109
The Keen of Hamar 109
The Knab 29
The Lodberries 29
The Old Haa Museum 95
The Original Cake Fridge 68
The Outpost 62
The Tolbooth 29
The White Wife 95
time 127
Tingwall 56
tipping 127
Toft 78

toilets 128
tourist information 128
Tresta Beach 101
Trondra 61

U

Underhoull 108
Unst 104
Unst Boat Haven 110
Unst Heritage Centre 110
Unst Viking Project 110
Up Helly Aa 27, 117
Up Helly Aa Exhibition 28
Uyea Island 92
Uyeasound 104

V

Vaasetter 54
Vementry 65
Vidlin 75
Voe 78

W

Walls 71
Ward Hill 54
Ward of Bressay 35
Ward of Clett 82
weather and climate 6
Weaving Shed Gallery 87
West Burrafirth 68
Westerwick Beach 72
West Sandwick 97
Westside 64
West Voe Beach 49
Whalsay 80
Whalsay Golf Club 84
Whalsay Heritage Centre 81
Windhouse 97
Wild Skies Trail 5, 112
Wool Week 117

Y

Yell 94